D0481329

Wenceslas Square

WENCESLAS SQUARE

By
Larry Shue

GARDEN CITY, NEW YORK

Design by Maria Chiarino
Manufactured in the United States of America
Photographs by Carol Rosegg/Martha Swope Associates

Quality Printing and Binding by:
Berryville Graphics
P.O. Box 272
Berryville, VA 22611 U.S.A.

WENCESLAS SQUARE
Originally produced by
The Apollo Group and Paramount Pictures
for *The Chicago Theater Project*

Original New York production by
New York Shakespeare Festival
Produced by Joseph Papp

WENCESLAS SQUARE was presented by the New York Shakespeare Festival (Joseph Papp, President) at the Public/ Martinson Hall Theatre in New York City on March 2, 1988. It was directed by Jerry Zaks; the set design was by Loren Sherman; the costume design was by William Ivey Long; the lighting design was by Paul Gallo; the casting was by Rosemarie Tichler/James Mulkin; and the associate producer was Jason Steven Cohen. The cast, in order of appearance, was as follows:

THE MEN .... Victor Garber
VINCE COREY .... Jonathan Hadary
DOOLEY .... Bruce Norris
THE WOMEN .... Dana Ivey

WENCESLAS SQUARE is designed to be performed with two card tables, four chairs, and whatever props and costumes seem necessary. Also, to use only four actors, as follows—

Vince Corey, PhD—*A College professor, mid-thirties*

Bob Dooley—*A student, early twenties*

An Actor (referred to as "A")—*Plays the narrator (an older Bob Dooley), as well as a number of Czech men—waiters, actors, students, a madman, a construction worker*

An Actress—*Plays several Czech women—an executive secretary at the National Museum, an old translator, a young interpreter*

WENCESLAS SQUARE

ACT I

NARRATOR *(appears in light, C)*: I am mankind. *(To the audience)* Not really. I just wanted to scare you there, a little bit. Really, my name's Bob Dooley; some of you know me already. I work here. Well, here, Milwaukee, St. Louis. Design lights, design sets. *(Pointing to the two coffee tables)* This is some of my work. What do you think? *(Crossing to the tables)* I'll give you a tour of the set, here. *(He turns one table on its side, back facing us. The other he leaves upright in front of it)* This is a booth in the dining car of a European train. 1974. Pretty obvious, I know. The old, polished wood, the plush seats. . . . Here's a window; outside, farmlands gliding by, furrows in the frosted ground, vineyards. Tall forests of birch and pine. Rugged country. See, I'd never travelled, really. Oh, in the army, a little, but I'd gone right back home to finish school on my G.I. Bill. Heverly College. Cementville, Indiana. Yes, there is. I was studying to be a dental ceramacist, at the time. I figured, you know—life is uncertain, governments change, fortunes rise and fall, but if there's one thing you can count on, it's false teeth. Oh, and also, I was sort of photographer for the school paper. Second-stringer, no big deal. So naturally, here I was sitting on a train thundering into Czechoslovakia. *You're* wondering. *I* was wondering. (DOOLEY *and* VINCE *have entered and sat at the table)* That's me with the camera.

VINCE *(looking out the window)*: Look at this. Chekhov country.

DOOLEY: Yeah? . . .

VINCE: Look at those woods. I bet they're just full of deer.

DOOLEY: Yep.

VINCE: Let's kill 'em.

DOOLEY: Sure.

NARRATOR: The other guy is Vince Corey, head of the theatre department at Heverly. *Doc*tor Vince Corey. I was taking his English Drama class for the credit, and spent most of my time wondering how he had become a doctor. He didn't like to read, he used to skip faculty meetings. He even cut classes. He was a good theatre director, people said, and I could believe that—the way he was always leaping into things, coercing and charming people, creating projects off the top of his head and, somehow, pulling them off. But I mean, nobody would have accused him of being a scholar—so when I found out he'd written this *book*—He had written a book about the Czech theatre after the Soviet takeover of '68. It was about to be published, in June. Vince was getting a free trip back to Prague, in fact, to do a final chapter on the thing—and one day he asked me if I'd like to go along as photographer. They had the money, he said. I can't remember—I must have said "Yes."

VINCE: Wait'll you see Prague. I mean, for Central Europe, it's very fancy. But there's, like, one of everything. Every year, in all the stores, there's—this year's winter coat. Green.

DOOLEY: Uh-huh.

VINCE: And one car. The Skoda. On the streets, you want a snack, there's guys selling popcorn. No salt, no butter, nothin'. Couple of feathers in it, y'know? Some rocks at the bottom? It's great. Oh—you got the gum and cigarettes?

DOOLEY: Yeah.

VINCE: You did?

DOOLEY: Yeah.

VINCE: Good. Good. You'll be glad you did that.

DOOLEY: I didn't think I had a choice.

VINCE: Hm?

DOOLEY: I mean, you sort of made it sound like they wouldn't let me across the border if I didn't have ten dollars worth of chewing gum.

VINCE: No it'll be great. Be great, you'll see. Little kids come up to you? You got a stick of gum, you can lead 'em all into the river. It's great. And, oh—guys'll come up wanting you to change money?

DOOLEY: Yeah?

VINCE: Yeah, but don't do it. It's black market. You wind up in jail.

DOOLEY *(a little worried)*: Okay . . .

VINCE: A lot of those guys are informers, anyway. For the government.

DOOLEY: How do they know you're an American?

VINCE: Are you kidding? You stick out a mile. You're the only—you're the one not wearing the green winter coat.

DOOLEY: Oh.

VINCE: Listen—see if this is all right with you. I was thinking we should look up Ladislav and Katya; maybe they'll put us up for the week.

DOOLEY: Now these are—?

VINCE: Katya was my translator. Interpreter.

DOOLEY: Right.

VINCE: Really smart. Good English. And Ladislav's her husband.

DOOLEY: Uh-huh.

VINCE: Also very smart. Not-so-good English.

DOOLEY: Uh-huh. All right.

VINCE: But—see, we're supposed to register with the police, tell 'em where we're staying? But I don't want to, not if we're at Lad and Katya's. I just don't want their names on anything.

DOOLEY: Okay. And—we can get away with that, you think?

VINCE: How do I know?

DOOLEY: Well—Doctor Corey, if—

VINCE: Hey. Vince, okay?

DOOLEY: Yeah. Okay—

VINCE: And who do you want to be? Robert? Rob?

DOOLEY: It—doesn't matter—

VINCE: Great.

DOOLEY: Now, if—

VINCE: How 'bout "Flash"?

DOOLEY: Uh, how 'bout "Dooley"?

VINCE: Dooley. *(Noticing someone—actor "A" as a border guard—approaching)* Woop! Heads up. You got your passport?

DOOLEY: Yeah?

VINCE: Friendly border guard type, here.

DOOLEY: He looks—is he *Russian*?

VINCE: You got me.

BORDER GUARD *(entering)*: *Pasy, prosim.* [Passports, please.] (VINCE *hands him his passport. The guard looks at it a long time, studies* VINCE's *face, then the passport again. He returns it, and repeats the process with* DOOLEY) Thank you. *(Exits)*

VINCE: Are you all right?

DOOLEY: Sure.

VINCE: Good.

DOOLEY: A change of underwear—I'll be fine. (VINCE *laughs)* Look, can I ask you something?

VINCE: Sure.

DOOLEY: It's just that—I'm not quite sure—

VINCE: What?

DOOLEY: Why are we here?

VINCE: What, theologically speaking?

DOOLEY: No—

VINCE: I know. All right. Well, *I'm* here, the publisher wants me to do a final chapter, "Where Are They Now?" Talk to everyone I saw before, get an update on all their projects. So on?

DOOLEY: Yeah?

VINCE: And *you're* here, you're gonna get pictures, right? Performances, uh—I guess, informal portraits of everyone?

DOOLEY: Sure, but—why me? I mean, the school has a photography department. You could've had—*(Shrugs)*

VINCE: Yeah, buncha jerks. You know. I guess—I liked the way you talked to my class.

DOOLEY: Oh. *(They watch out the window a moment)* I don't remember ever saying anything in your class.

VINCE: Right.

DOOLEY: Oh.

VINCE: Plus, you can spell. You know? I don't know. People that can spell. I just think somebody that can spell oughta see this shit.

DOOLEY: Oh . . .

VINCE: Okay?

DOOLEY: Yeah. Just curious. I mean—suddenly here I am, a long way from home, I just thought—

VINCE: Look, do me one favor, will you? This trip? Don't call Cementville, Indiana "home," all right?

DOOLEY: Why not?

VINCE: Just—it bugs me, all right?

DOOLEY: I don't know why everybody makes fun of Cementville.

VINCE: Have you ever been anywhere else?

DOOLEY: Sure.

VINCE: I don't mean Terre Haute.

DOOLEY: All right, then. No.

VINCE: I tell you one thing. If this books sells at *all*, I am getting outta there. I gotta find some school where the administration reads without moving its lips.

DOOLEY: How many copies have to sell, for you to be able to move?

VINCE: Five.

DOOLEY: *Five?*

VINCE: Or, all right, let's be realistic. Four.

DOOLEY: Big money, huh?

VINCE: It's not money. It's leverage. You publish a book, you can write your own ticket. You can pick your school, you can—you can get the hell out of Cementville, Indiana. I don't want my kids to grow up in Cementville, Indiana. I know you love it.

DOOLEY: So that's why you wrote the book? To get out?

VINCE: No. I wrote the book—you really want to know?

DOOLEY: Yeah.

VINCE: Okay. I just—I found myself in the middle of something that was fantastic. It was right after the takeover. Right after the Prague Spring. You know about Dubcek?

DOOLEY: Uh—

VINCE: Their president.

DOOLEY: Oh—

VINCE: Or, not their—but their—prime minister, sort of thing.

DOOLEY: Right?

VINCE: And he was this—first, okay. You gotta remember that these people, they're right in the middle. Central Europe. And they keep getting *besieged* by everybody. For centuries. I mean, the Poles, the Nazis, the Russians —you name it. So in '68—*some*how—the Russians let 'em elect this guy Dubcek, who happened to believe in intellectual *freed*om. Well—so suddenly, people found that they could write again, they could publish, they could paint, they could express themselves again. The place went nuts. Prague? There was this—flowering. This optimistic, brilliant time. I just missed it.

DOOLEY: So the Russians just kind of—

VINCE: Oh, yeah. You know them. Got a little nervous about it all, sent in the tanks. Right into the middle of Prague, shut it right down. Trains, telephones, TV, the arts. Dead. Stopped. Martial law. So by the time I got there, and I was just—Sarah was doing her master's on European architecture, so we got cleared for a visit, and I was just—*along*, y'know? And I started going to *plays*. Dooley?—well, you'll see. You don't have to understand a word. You can see what they're doing. They take a classic—something that'll be approved by the censors—and they'll do it politically. So that it's *so clear* we're not—we're not talking about Montagues and Capulets, we're talking about the Czechs and the Poles. Y'know? Or they do little comedy revues, at the Semafor, the Cinohernyi Klub, little places, dumb little skits and you're laughing, and you realize halfway through that the dancing wolf with the boots on is probably Russia. Which is what everyone else has been laughing at all along. You see? It's great stuff— and dangerous. Walking that line. But—fantastic. And *every*body goes. That's the thing. They can't have public meetings anymore. So *every*body goes to the theatre. It's fantastic.

DOOLEY: Huh.

VINCE: I saw that. I—I knew. Somebody had to write a book about it.

DOOLEY: Yeah?

VINCE: And I—I'll never write another one. I know that. But—when you see these people's com*mit*ment. And you know that, for them, life without commitment is a bagful of shit.

DOOLEY *(smiling)*: Lovely thought.

VINCE: Like that?

DOOLEY: Yeah.

VINCE: Old Czech expression.

DOOLEY: Uh-huh.

VINCE: Suffers in translation, a little.

DOOLEY: Yeah.

VINCE: *Boy,* I feel good. Yep. This feels right. You get old fast in Cementville. You know? Okay—first we're gonna—we'll go see Pavlicek. You're gonna love Pavlicek. Fucker knows every bar in town, speaks five languages, acts, directs. Plus he runs the National Theatre.

DOOLEY: Wow.

VINCE: He did a production of *Fiddler on the Roof.* You believe that? He convinced 'em it was a glorification of the Russian people, so they let him do *Fiddler on the Roof.*

DOOLEY: Hm.

VINCE: Nifty guy.

DOOLEY: Now, what's his name?

VINCE: Nikolai Pavlicek. Nickey's named after him. Sarah doesn't know it.

DOOLEY: All these names.

VINCE: I know. You'll get 'em. *(Seeing "A" offstage, as waiter)* Hey, *there's* a waiter. Finally. You want a beer? Let's get a beer, okay?

DOOLEY: Whatever you say.

VINCE: Hey, you wanta order in Czech? *Dve piva,* tell him.

DOOLEY: No, really, I—.

VINCE: Come *on.* It's not hard. Just say, *Dve piva.* *("A" enters, white towel over one arm, as a waiter.* VINCE *signals him, then nudges* DOOLEY)

DOOLEY *(to the waiter)*: Uh—*Dve piva.*

WAITER *(austrian accent, imperiously)*: Two beers, very good, gentlemen. *(He exits.* DOOLEY *sighs)*

VINCE: You wanta learn some more Czech?

DOOLEY: Not now, thanks.

VINCE: *Dobrou notz?*

DOOLEY: Really. I—.

VINCE: Come *on. Dobrou notz?* Means, "Good night?" Come on.

DOOLEY: *Dobrou notz?*

VINCE: "Good night." That was perfect.

DOOLEY: Fine. Could we stop, now?

VINCE: Oh, we have to. That's all the Czech I know.

DOOLEY: That's *all?* (VINCE *shrugs happily)* How did you get around, when you were here?

VINCE: I had an interpreter.

DOOLEY: All the time?

VINCE: Not all the time.

DOOLEY: What did you do when you didn't?

VINCE: I had two beers and said good night. *(Light change. The actors change the scene,* VINCE *and* DOOLEY, *suitcases in hand, acting out some of the following.* DOOLEY *stops for an occasional photo)*

NARRATOR: The next day, there we were, stone sidewalks underfoot, clattering with luggage toward Ladislav and Katya's place. Prague. *Praha,* they call it. Around us and beyond us, cathedral spires, gray government buildings. Store windows with signs inside, proclaiming indecipherable bargains.

VINCE *(as they walk)*: It's unbelievable. Look how high the prices are now. And those *coats.* Fake fur? Five years ago there was nothin' like that. And look here—Coca-Cola. Incredible. *("A" reenters as a bum)*

BUM: Money? Change money?

DOOLEY: *No! ("A" disappears fearfully)*

VINCE: That was good.

DOOLEY: I didn't mean to scare the guy.

VINCE: That's all right, though. You remembered.

DOOLEY: What's "no" in Czech?

VINCE: I don't know. "Yes" is—is *ano*, I remember that.

DOOLEY: "Aa-no."

VINCE: Yes.

DOOLEY: "Aaa-no." *(They walk off)*

NARRATOR: We found them at home—student-type hous-
ing, lots of books, three rooms and a kitchen. Katya
was pretty and pregnant, and *very* serious; Ladislav
was trying to grow a goatee and to improve his English,
with about equal success. Surprised exclamations and
then, as Vince had predicted, we were offered a place
to stay.

KATYA *(emerging from doorway)*: The room—it is all
right?

VINCE: It's just great.

KATYA: I'm afraid it's not—American enough.

VINCE: We like it.

DOOLEY: Sure. I haven't slept in a bunk bed since I was
thirteen.

KATYA: It's too small?

DOOLEY: No! It's—fine.

KATYA: I hope it's American enough.

DOOLEY: No, it's—really.

KATYA *(with tea tray)*: Some tea?

VINCE: Uh, sure.

KATYA: I hope it's of a type you enjoy. I don't remember which.

VINCE: It'll be fine.

KATYA: Cream? Sugar? Both, yes?

VINCE: Yes. You remembered.

KATYA *(to DOOLEY)*: And you? Cream? Sugar?

DOOLEY: No. Neither.

KATYA: Do you drink—with lemon?

DOOLEY *(lying)*: No.

KATYA: We have no lemon.

DOOLEY: No, this is—perfect.

VINCE: Come on, have a seat.

KATYA: Eh?

VINCE: Sit.

KATYA: Yes. Good. *(Sits)* Would you prefer coffee?

VINCE: No. This is just fine.

DOOLEY: I enjoyed meeting Ladislav.

KATYA: Yes. Ladislav will return soon with—beer.

VINCE: Ah. Beer, huh?

KATYA: Yes.

VINCE: Oh, boy.

KATYA: Yes. *(Pause)* It's of poor quality.

VINCE: Great.

KATYA: Great?

VINCE: Sure.

KATYA: You enjoy—beer of poor quality?

VINCE: It's my favorite.

KATYA *(surprised)*: Ah! *(Shaking her head solemnly)* You always make me laugh.

VINCE *(smiles. Goes into briefcase)*: Here. I want to show you this. *(He hands her a stack of galley sheets)*

KATYA: Ah! This is—your book?

VINCE: Yes. Your book, too.

KATYA: No.

VINCE: Sure. Here. Look.

KATYA *(reading)*: "With special thanks to—my interpreter, Katya Daneshova, who—." Oh.

VINCE: All right?

KATYA *(looking at the page, frowning)*: It's—very kind.

VINCE: But?

KATYA: I am—angry with myself.

VINCE: No, don't be angry with yourself. But, what—the university wouldn't approve?

KATYA: It's impossible.

VINCE: All right. I just wanted you to know how much your help meant to me. You know? I'll take it out.

KATYA *(looking at the page)*: But—I will—always remember this sentence.

VINCE: Good. That's good. *(Actor "A," as* LADISLAV,*enters with stoppered beer bottles)*

LADISLAV: The cold. Hello!

VINCE: Ladislav! *(Getting the door)*

DOOLEY: Hi!

LADISLAV: The cold is—larger. Better.

VINCE: What?

LADISLAV: No. *More.* More cold.

VINCE: It's getting colder.

LADISLAV *(delighted)*: It's getting colder! Yes. It's getting colder. English.

VINCE: Yeah, it's tough.

LADISLAV: Hm?

VINCE: English. Difficult.

LADISLAV: Difficult! Yes! "It's getting colder."

KATYA: Yes.

LADISLAV: What is getting colder? *It* is getting colder. *(Shakes head)*

VINCE: Yeah. I know.

KATYA *(taking the bottles)*: Some beer?

VINCE: Sure. Thank you.

DOOLEY: Thanks.

LADISLAV: English—my English—has grown—down.

VINCE: We'd say, "My English is rusty."

LADISLAV: "Rusty"?

VINCE: Yeah.

LADISLAV *(with dictionary)*: Rusty. Hm. R—A?

DOOLEY: R—*U.*

LADISLAV: R—U—

DOOLEY: S—T—Y. Rusty.

LADISLAV: Rusty.

VINCE: Figure of speech.

LADISLAV *(reading)*: Rusty—"brown from oxidation."

VINCE: Well, yeah.

LADISLAV *(smiling)*: My English is brown from oxidation.

VINCE: Literally, yeah. But we wouldn't say that.

LADISLAV: My English is rusty.

VINCE & DOOLEY: Right.

LADISLAV: Right. I will learn.

VINCE: You're doing fine.

LADISLAV: I am doing fine.

VINCE: Yep.

LADISLAV: Good. Now—shall we eat the beer?

VINCE: Drink.

LADISLAV: Shall we eat—the drink?

VINCE: No. Shall we drink—the beer.

LADISLAV: Shall we drink the beer! Ah. Stupid.

VINCE: No! Not at all. Very good.

LADISLAV: No. I believe, no.

VINCE: *Yes. (Pointing) Your* English—yes—?

LADISLAV: I am English.

VINCE: No. I mean—*your* English—is *bet*ter—than *my Czech.*

LADISLAV: Ah!

VINCE: *I* can speak—

LADISLAV: Yes?

VINCE: I can speak—only two sentences, in Czech.

LADISLAV: Yes?

VINCE: *Dobroa notz?*

LADISLAV: Yes?

VINCE: And—*Dve piva.*

LADISLAV: Ah! *Dve piva.* Very good!

VINCE: But that's *all.*

LADISLAV: Hah?

VINCE: *Dobroa notz. Dve piva. No more.*

LADISLAV: You—your—Czech—is—rusty.

VINCE: Very rusty. Yes.

LADISLAV: Yes. So. *(Serving)* Now, we drink beer?

VINCE: Drink beer.

LADISLAV: And—soon? My English—and—your Czech. *Bet*ter.

VINCE: Beer will improve your English and my Czech.

LADISLAV: Yes!

VINCE: Very wise.

LADISLAV: Yes. Who?

VINCE: You.

LADISLAV: No.

VINCE: Yes.

LADISLAV: No. But—we will speak—English? Each day?

VINCE: Yes. English every day.

KATYA: Some days—I cannot come with you. So—Lad will come.

VINCE: Good. That's good. (LAD *shrugs, smiles)* I want Dooley to see all of *Praha.*

KATYA: We will show you.

DOOLEY: Well, thank you.

VINCE: Dooley has brought lots of chewing gum.

KATYA: Yes?

VINCE: And cigarettes.

KATYA: Yes?

VINCE: To give to people in the street.

DOOLEY: Yes.

KATYA: To give?

VINCE: Yes. Children who ask for chewing gum? Men who
  want cigarettes?

KATYA: Ah! *(She translates for* LAD) *Chvee vaslee zhvee-*
  gachkee gooma a tseegarette. (He laughs) No. No more.

VINCE: No more? They don't do that anymore?

KATYA: No. Now—we have chewing gum.

VINCE: Yes? Cigarettes?

KATYA: We have them here. Yes. Now.

VINCE: Hm.

KATYA: Many new things. Clothing. Tobacco. Nightclubs?

VINCE: *Night*clubs.

KATYA: Yes. Many—improvements.

VINCE: I *guess.* Yeah.

KATYA *(to* DOOLEY, *concerned)*: How many—how much
  chewing gum and cigarettes—did you bring?

DOOLEY: Oh, about ten pounds.

KATYA: Ten?

VINCE: Pounds. About half a suitcase full.

KATYA: Half? Half a suitcase?

VINCE: Yep.

KATYA: Ah! *(Looks at* DOOLEY, *then translates for* LAD) *Chvee vaslee yenom pool koofroo cheegacheck a tseegaret.*

LADISLAV: Ah! Yes? (DOOLEY *shrugs)* Mm.

KATYA: I don't know—what you will do—with so much chewing gum. (DOOLEY *shrugs again)*

VINCE: No? We blew it, I guess.

DOOLEY: It's all right.

KATYA: So much chewing gum.

LADISLAV: Yes. *(Shakes head)*

KATYA: It's—a grave question.

VINCE: Mmm. *(Blackout. "A" steps forward into light)*

NARRATOR: The following morning, bright and cold, onto the streets again. Off to the National Museum to surprise Vince's friend, Illinova.

DOOLEY *(as they enter)*: Who?

VINCE: Illinova. Dynamite lady. Secretary at the National Museum, knows everybody. Lozek's her brother-in-law. I told you about Lozek?

DOOLEY: Uh—

VINCE: The old actor, at the National Theatre.

DOOLEY: Right.

VINCE: Oh look, the castle.

DOOLEY: Wow. What are they?

VINCE: Castle guards.

DOOLEY: AK-47's.

VINCE: What?

DOOLEY: Russian rifles.

VINCE: Yeah?

DOOLEY: Yep.

VINCE *(as they exit)*: Want a frozen banana?

DOOLEY: Nope.

VINCE: My treat.

DOOLEY: Nope. *(They exit. Lights up on* ILLINOVA *in her "office"—desk, papers, telephone)*

ILLINOVA *(on the phone, in Czech)*: Illinova? *(Pause) Neh, taw beela beestava za Brateeslava. Hoodabnee nas-troye mameh vaskladoo. Naskhladano.* [No, sir, that was a temporary exhibit from Bratislava. The only musical instruments in our permanent collection are in storage. You're welcome.] *(Hangs up. A knock at the door) Dahleh* [Come in.](VINCE *and* DOOLEY *enter,* VINCE *grinning. She stands, taking off her glasses, which are on a cord around her neck) Aah! (She is a little embar-*

rassed. ILLINOVA *does not lose her composure, as a rule)* My God.

VINCE: Are you busy?

ILLINOVA: Come in, please. Vince. My God.

VINCE: Are you surprised?

ILLINOVA: Yes. I think so, yes. They said two *Anglichany*— English gentlemen—so I thought—who? (VINCE *laughs)* I couldn't think.

VINCE: And this is Bob Dooley?

DOOLEY *(shaking hands)*: Hello.

ILLINOVA: Bob?

VINCE: We call him Dooley.

ILLINOVA: His surname?

VINCE: Right. We call him by his surname.

ILLINOVA: As in Czech.

VINCE: What? As in Czech. That's right. Same thing.

ILLINOVA: Well—my God. (VINCE *laughs)* You always overwhelm me.

VINCE: Yep.

ILLINOVA: And how is dear Sarah?

VINCE: Sarah's fine. The kids are great.

ILLINOVA: The children! How old are they now?

VINCE: Uh—keeps *chang*ing. I think—six, and—four. Is that right? That's right.

ILLINOVA *(shaking her head)*: Amazing.

VINCE: Yep.

ILLINOVA: Please. Sit. *(They do)* And, Dooley? Are you a student?

DOOLEY: Yes.

ILLINOVA: Yes? In which field of study?

DOOLEY: Well, I'm learning to be a dental ceramicist.

ILLINOVA: A—?

DOOLEY: I'm—learning to make false teeth.

ILLINOVA: Ah!

DOOLEY: Yeah.

ILLINOVA: False *teeth.*

DOOLEY: Yes.

VINCE: Also—good photographer.

ILLINOVA: Yes?

VINCE: He's doing the photographs for my book.

ILLINOVA: Your book! A new book?

VINCE: No, same book. *(Hands her galley sheets from his attaché)* Here.

ILLINOVA *(taking the galleys)*: This is astonishing. You simply walk through the door—. *(Looking at the galleys)* Ah. Just look!

VINCE: It's coming out in June.

ILLINOVA: June. Imagine.

VINCE: But I've got to do one more chapter. So I want to see everyone here that I saw before.

ILLINOVA: I see. *(Pause)* How long are you here?

VINCE: One week.

ILLINOVA: One week. Have you seen Lozek?

VINCE: No. We just got here. *(To DOOLEY)* Lozek's the old actor I told you about.

ILLINOVA: My husband's brother.

VINCE: Is he, is he acting now?

ILLINOVA: Oh, yes. In *Hamlet.*

VINCE: *Hamlet?* At the National?

ILLINOVA: Yes. He is the grave digger.

DOOLEY: Oh, yes.

ILLINOVA: He's quite good, of course.

VINCE: Sure. How's the production?

ILLINOVA *(shakes head)*: Not very good.

VINCE: Why?

ILLINOVA: The director I think.

VINCE: Oh?

ILLINOVA: A new—attempt. The director must always see things through new eyes. And sometimes these eyes are too new for Shakespeare.

VINCE: Yes. Who directed it, Pavlicek?

ILLINOVA: I think—not.

VINCE: How about Langer, is he in it?

ILLINOVA: Jiri Langer? No. No, I believe he's performing in Bratislava now. Or one of the provinces.

VINCE: The provinces? Jiri Langer? Why isn't he here playing Hamlet?

ILLINOVA: Who can know the mind of a director?

VINCE: I suppose. So what else is on in town? That you, uh—

ILLINOVA *(glasses on, consulting a schedule)*: Really—I can't advise you. Cinohernyi Klub—not performing. Semafor—a program of popular songs.

VINCE: Popular songs? The *Sem*afor?

ILLINOVA: Yes.

VINCE: Hm.

ILLINOVA: Really, it's a bad time.

VINCE: Anything else?

ILLINOVA: Also the National—a new Russian play. I haven't seen it, but—not so very good, they tell me.

VINCE: The last Russian play I saw there, they had a tractor on the stage.

ILLINOVA *(nods)*: This is similar, I think.

VINCE: Well—we'll find something. Go to see Lozek anyway.

ILLINOVA: And who else will you see?

VINCE: Everyone that I saw before, I hope. I'll need your help, again.

ILLINOVA *(writing)*: Of course.

VINCE: You know. Swoboda, the designer. And Vanek—

ILLINOVA: Yes. Let me know when you have—difficulty.

VINCE: Oh, I sure will. Oh, and I really want to see Smocekova. And Jiri Langer. And Pavlicek, of course, but I'll—don't worry about him.

ILLINOVA *(stops writing)*: Perhaps you won't be able to see —all.

VINCE: Well—try, anyway.

ILLINOVA: Only a week. It's not so long.

VINCE: I know.

ILLINOVA: Will you take some time to enjoy *Praha,* do you think?

VINCE: Oh, sure.

ILLINOVA: "Oh, sure." But you must.

VINCE: We will.

ILLINOVA: Yes, but I know you. *(To* DOOLEY) He never looks. He rushes here and there, talking to people, rushing home again to write. *(To* VINCE) You should walk along the river, a little.

VINCE: Yes.

ILLINOVA: If you don't, you'll drive yourself to madness. Like Kafka.

VINCE: I will. I promise.

ILLINOVA: If so, I'll see which of these names I can find for you. Yes?

VINCE: Great. Yes. *(To* DOOLEY) I told you she was fabulous.

ILLINOVA: Fabulous?

VINCE: Fabulous. You know that word?

ILLINOVA: Yes. Fabulous. It means—imaginary.

VINCE: Imaginary? No. It means—wonderful.

ILLINOVA: Ah.

VINCE: No. I didn't mean you were imaginary.

ILLINOVA: It seemed—an odd compliment.

VINCE: Yeah. No. Anyway—*(Rising)* You're busy.

ILLINOVA: I'm never too busy for you to visit. Dooley?

DOOLEY: Goodbye. Thank you.

ILLINOVA: A great pleasure.

VINCE: And we'll see you tomorrow, right?

ILLINOVA: Yes. That will be—fabulous!

VINCE: Fabulous!

ILLINOVA: Fabulous! *(Light change.* VINCE *takes out a piece of paper. He and* DOOLEY *are now walking down a hall, reading door numbers)*

VINCE: This should be it somewhere. Fuckin' government buildings. I used to get lost every time I came here.

DOOLEY: Yeah. *(Reading)* Smocekova?

VINCE: Yeah.

DOOLEY: Isn't this—?

VINCE: This is it. *(Knocks)* Dinnertime, maybe. *(Knocks again)*

DOOLEY *(looking up)*: Austere sort of place.

VINCE: What?

DOOLEY: "Austere." Impressive but creepy.

VINCE: Yeah. Just—your friendly neighborhood library.

DOOLEY: Mm-hmm.

VINCE *(starts to write a note, then sees someone offstage)*: Um—hello? Do you speak English? *("A" enters with an attaché case. He observes them coolly, with a faint professional smile)*

MAN IN LIBRARY *(finally)*: Yes?

VINCE: We're looking for Mrs. Smocekova. Do you know when she'll be in?

MAN IN LIBRARY *(looks at* DOOLEY, *then at* VINCE): . . . Smocekova?

VINCE: Yes. She works here?

MAN IN LIBRARY *(again the smile)*: She is ill.

VINCE: Oh! Really? What—is it something serious?

MAN IN LIBRARY: May I help you?

VINCE: No. No, we were just—*(He stops)*

DOOLEY: Just visiting.

MAN IN LIBRARY *(nods)*: Visiting.

DOOLEY: Yeah.

VINCE: Just—some research.

MAN IN LIBRARY: Research. *(He seems to look at something far away for a few moments)* I see . . . And—your name?

VINCE: Well, no, that's—When is she expected back, do you know?

MAN IN LIBRARY *(quietly)*: No. She is ill.

VINCE: Hm.

MAN IN LIBRARY: Come, please—.

VINCE: No, no, don't bother, We'll—it's not important.

MAN IN LIBRARY *(seeing the notepad)*: You're leaving your number?

VINCE: Well—maybe we'll just try again tomorrow. *("A" looks at them)* Well—thank you for your help. *("A" looks at them)* Bye.

DOOLEY: Thank you. (VINCE *and* DOOLEY *exit. "A" watches them, then exits.* VINCE *and* DOOLEY *reenter, now on the street)*

VINCE: I wanted to get out of there.

DOOLEY: Why? What—?

VINCE: I don't know. I didn't like that guy. There was something going on there, I don't know what.

DOOLEY: What.

VINCE: I don't know, just a feeling. He wanted to know our names.

DOOLEY: Yeah.

VINCE: I don't know.

DOOLEY: Vince—I mean—how scared should I be? You know?

VINCE: You mean, of what? You mean—?

DOOLEY: I just mean—in general. How worried should we be, about being here?

VINCE: Naah, don't. We're all right. I mean, guys like that guy—I mean, there's always a certain number of human shits walking around. Right?

DOOLEY: Yeah?

VINCE: So you don't tell 'em anything, that's all. You just gotta watch it a little, y'know? Like what you say, or what—what you talk about in restaurants? So on? I mean—

DOOLEY: Restaurants?

VINCE: Yeah. I mean, not *all* of 'em. But I mean, you gotta figure, some of these places you're not only having lunch but you're also cutting an album.

DOOLEY: Gee.

VINCE: So you play it safe, right? But it's not—I mean, the Russians don't care about us.

DOOLEY: *Russ*ians.

VINCE: No, we are no big deal to them. Believe me. Here, *oh*—you can—*(They have stopped walking, and stand next to the two tables, stacked atop one another)* Get, let's climb up on this a second.

DOOLEY: What?

VINCE: Get up here, I'll show you something.

DOOLEY: Is it—safe?

VINCE: Sure. It's scaffold, right? It's for workers to stand on and—work.

DOOLEY: I know, but—

VINCE: Come *on*. I want to show you something. *(They climb up, sit)*

DOOLEY: Okayyy . . .

VINCE *(pointing)*: There. Look. See where we are? There's Illinova's place—

DOOLEY: Uh-huh.

VINCE: —the Museum. And Wenceslas Square?

DOOLEY: Wenceslas? Like the song?

VINCE: Sure.

DOOLEY: Who's the statue of?

VINCE: Two guesses.

DOOLEY: Wenceslas?

VINCE: Yep.

DOOLEY: *King* Wenceslas?

VINCE: No, this was Mel Wenceslas, he was a tailor from New Jersey. *(They watch for a moment. DOOLEY takes a picture)* So how about, you wanta meet over there at six?

DOOLEY: Front of the statue?

VINCE: Front of the statue.

DOOLEY: Fine.

VINCE: Right? *(They watch)* Man. The Russians have really fixed this place up, though. I'll give 'em that. Front of the Museum, when I left here in '70, was still just covered with bullet holes.

DOOLEY: From the takeover?

VINCE: Yep. Now it looks like nothing ever happened. Weird. And down there, by the statue? Where the flowers are now?

DOOLEY: Yeah?

VINCE: One night, while I was still here, there was this young student, Jan Palach. Set himself on fire. Right there.

DOOLEY: As a protest.

VINCE: Yeah. And—he didn't die right away. He hung on for a couple of days. Things got very quiet, everywhere. They told me to stay inside and not ask any questions about it. A lot of people stayed in, I think. Then word came around, finally, that he had—died. And—nobody said much. Everybody went back to work. But two days later, when they had the kid's funeral, ten thousand people joined the procession. Torchlit procession through the streets of Prague. It was eerie, and—I don't know.

DOOLEY: Yeah?

VINCE: It's hard to explain, the feeling. And that night, the night he died, the Semafor did a performance, one of their satirical revues. It was incredible. Somebody said to one of them, "How can we laugh?" And they said— "How can we not laugh?" *(DOOLEY nods. Suddenly a police whistle, very near, breaks the silence. Rough, loud commands, in Russian, from "A," offstage)*

RUSSIAN GUARD *(from offstage)*: Stoy! Stoy, dvor! [Stop! Stop, thief!]

VINCE: Down, let's get down. *(They start clambering down the "scaffold")*

DOOLEY: Oh, shit. *(More shouts, whistles)*

VINCE: We're okay. Just act stupid.

DOOLEY: Shit, shit. *(They are down)*

VINCE: Don't worry. Come on. You got your passport?

DOOLEY *(unable to find it)*: Uh—

VINCE: You'd better—

DOOLEY *(still searching)*: I don't—

VINCE: Uh—*(A hobbling, frightened old man—Actress in coat, galoshes, glasses, hat—enters from D., crossing up past DOOLEY and VINCE. As the old man reaches them, "A" emerges from the same entrance, as a Russian guard, rifle slung over one shoulder, in pursuit. He shouts and grabs the old man from behind, twisting his arm behind him)*

RUSSIAN GUARD: *Stoy! Dvor!*

OLD MAN: *Neh! Neh!* [No! No!]

RUSSIAN GUARD: *Beestro! Samnoy!* [Quickly! Come with me!] *(The old man struggles weakly, and the Russian turns him and hustles him quickly out)*

VINCE: Oh. You all right?

DOOLEY: I thought they were after us.

VINCE: I know.

DOOLEY: A little, uh—

VINCE: Yep.

DOOLEY: What was going on?

VINCE: I don't know.

DOOLEY: What was that guy, a guard?

VINCE: Police, I think.

DOOLEY: A policeman?

VINCE: Yeah?

DOOLEY: That poor old man. I wonder what he did?

VINCE: I don't know. Something. Money changer? Thief?

DOOLEY: Gee.

VINCE: Hey. Nothing we can do.

DOOLEY: No.

VINCE: You okay?

DOOLEY: Yeah.

VINCE: You found your passport.

DOOLEY *(pocketing it again)*: Yeah.

VINCE: What do you want? You wanta get a drink?

DOOLEY: Yeah. *(They start off)* No. No. Go ahead. You've got stuff—

VINCE: No, hell—

DOOLEY: No go ahead. Really. I want to get some shots.

VINCE: Okay. *(Pause)* I mean—you know, we might as well assume he was a crook. I mean, there's nothing—

DOOLEY: No, I know. No, you're right.

VINCE: Okay. Six o'clock, then.

DOOLEY: Six o'clock.

VINCE: Hold on to your passport.

DOOLEY *(smiles)*: I will. *(With a wave, VINCE is gone)*

NARRATOR *(entering, to audience)*: I wandered toward the Square, thinking about the old guy. I took some pictures of the famous clock, a tailor shop, some strange old cars. Inside a new arcade, I watched a film crew make a movie. Just one scene, over and over. A pretty woman passed in front of me. She smiled, I took her picture, and she thanked me—and I realized she was a man in drag. *(Sounds of children playing)* Some kids were playing kickball in the street—their language making every happy shout end in a kind of cry. I took their pictures. *(A ball comes rolling onto the stage.* DOOLEY *kicks it back off, with a laugh)* I offered them some gum, but they didn't care for any. I followed them for blocks, getting myself a needed dose of innocence. I stopped to change to Polaroid flash, looked up, and they were gone. Curfew time, I guessed. I looked at my watch in the fading light. It was late. I headed back but soon I knew that I was lost. *(As young* DOOLEY*)*

DOOLEY: Oh, great. Great.

NARRATOR: I decided to stay on lighted streets and take a taxi.

DOOLEY: Okay. Hey.

NARRATOR: But there were no taxis. There were no cars. I walked and walked, farther and farther. Not a soul in sight.

DOOLEY: Great. Middle of Prague.

NARRATOR: Gray apartment blocks gave way to rubble-filled lots. Darkening alleyways, silent factories. I kept to the lighted streets. At eight-thirty, they turned off the streetlights. *(The stage is plunged into darkness. "A" exits)*

DOOLEY: Great. Oh, boy. *(Pause)* What I *don't* want is a policeman. *(Pause)* Fuck. *(Another moment. Then, far U., someone's breath is heard being expelled in a hiss. Pause)* Hello? *(Pause)* Someone there? *(Pause)*

MADMAN *("A," whispered)*: Anglitsky . . . *(Pause)*

DOOLEY: Hello?

MADMAN: *Preshel sas podeevat, kocheechko?* [Have you come to visit me?]

DOOLEY: Hello? Uh—do you know—Wenceslas Square? I'm trying to find *Wenceslas Square.*

MADMAN: Too late . . .

DOOLEY: You speak English? I'm trying to find a taxi. *Taxi? (Pause)* I—I've been looking for somebody for—for *hours,* but I—so far, I've found—*no*body . . .

MADMAN: Yes. You have found nobody . . .

DOOLEY: Can you help me? *(Pause)* Can you help me get a taxi? *(Pause. Starts off. Stops)*

MADMAN: A taxi? A taxi, you want?

DOOLEY: That's all I want.

MADMAN: All you want.

DOOLEY: Yes.

MADMAN: Very wise. *(Pause)*

DOOLEY: Bye. *(He starts off again)*

MADMAN: No! There is no taxi there.

DOOLEY *(stopped again)*: All right. Can you tell me—?

MADMAN: That way is only prison. Do you want it? Do you want prison?

LADISLAV: English—my English—has grown—down.

VINCE: We'd say, "My English is rusty."

LADISLAV *(with dictionary . . . reading)*: Rusty—"brown from oxidation." *(Smiling)* My English is brown from oxidation.

VINCE: Literally, yeah. But we wouldn't say that.

LADISLAV: My English is rusty. . . . Good. Now—shall we eat the beer?

VINCE: Drink.

LADISLAV: Shall we eat—the drink?

At left, Victor Garber with (standing) Jonathan Hadary and (seated, from left to right) Bruce Norris and Dana Ivey

Photo Credit: Martha Swope Associates/Carol Rosegg

SMOCEKOVA: I'm forbidden to translate. . . . We translate. We use fictitious names. Mad, isn't it. The state still requires our services, but we must use pseudonyms. Sometimes, they even give me my own forbidden translations, to retranslate. It's mad.

At left, Dana Ivey with Bruce Norris

Photo Credit: Martha Swope Associates/Carol Rosegg

VINCE: So your beliefs are that all these people's heads are on the chopping block waiting for my book to come out. But *my* decision, right? Wonderful. . . . Is it possible, do you think . . . is it possible that you—are more afraid than is necessary?

KATYA: Yes, we are more afraid than is necessary. . . . Those who are less afraid than is necessary are no longer here.

From left to right, Dana Ivey, Victor Garber, Jonathan Hadary and Bruce Norris

Photo Credit: Martha Swope Associates/Carol Rosegg

VINCE: So! Well! Hey! Let's see here. We haven't seen any theatre, I've lost most of my friends, and I'm not publishing the book. We've accomplished a hell of a lot, this trip. . . . Would you tell somebody about this, someday? Cause that's the thing, really. Cause now nobody's gonna *know* about all this. So if you could just tell somebody.

At left, Bruce Norris with Jonathan Hadary

Photo Credit: Martha Swope Associates/Carol Rosegg

DOOLEY: No—

MADMAN: No? Then you must wait.

DOOLEY: Look, I don't want any trouble—

MADMAN *(approaching* DOOLEY): I will not eat your skin, English. Nor skin of milk. I will not eat it. *(Pause)*

DOOLEY: Good.

MADMAN: Do you want of mine? Do you want to eat it? No. Too late. Do you want my eyes? Do you want my teeth? Do you want my bones? Do you want my pus? *(Pause)*

DOOLEY: Just a taxi.

MADMAN: Too late. Too late.

DOOLEY: Look—

MADMAN: Ss! No! Do not—touch me.

DOOLEY: I won't.

MADMAN: No. Never must you touch. Or else my dreams may come to you.

DOOLEY: Look. I just—

MADMAN: Do you know me?

DOOLEY: No.

MADMAN: Have you ever spoken to the dead?

DOOLEY: No.

MADMAN: Yes. Now.

DOOLEY: No.

MADMAN: Once I could become many things. Each animal. But now no more. Worms eat them now.

DOOLEY: Uh—

MADMAN: Gone. They are gone. Oh. Be fearful of the beautiful stranger. Oh, English. Sleep with beautiful stranger, your animals may die.

DOOLEY: All right. I'm going to go. Now.

MADMAN: No.

DOOLEY: Yes.

MADMAN: No.

DOOLEY: I don't want any trouble—

MADMAN: *No.*

DOOLEY: Look. *(Pause)* You want some money?

MADMAN: No.

DOOLEY: Uh . . . you want—some *gum?* *(Pause)* Look. Look. *Cam*era. Polaroid. I'll leave it. I'll leave it here if you'll just—

MADMAN: Yes.

DOOLEY: The—okay? The camera?

MADMAN: Take the picture. *(Pause)*

DOOLEY: You want—you want me to take your picture?

MADMAN: Take the picture of death. *(Pause)*

DOOLEY: Uh . . . Okay. Stay there. I'm gonna take your picture . . . then I'm gonna leave. Okay? *(Pause. "A" begins to laugh quietly)* Okay? . . . *("A" laughs) All right—(A camera flash lights "A" 's grinning face for a second. His laughter swells, filling the night. From another part of the stage—*LAD *and* KATYA's *place—more laughter—loud, drunk, convivial. Lights up on the apartment, where* LAD, KATYA, VINCE *and* DOOLEY *sprawl about, having a fine, hilarious time. Even* KATYA *smiles a little)*

VINCE *(through laughter)*: So, again. You ran.

DOOLEY: Ran. Ran like hell.

VINCE: Sure. *(They laugh)* And the Square was two blocks away.

DOOLEY: About two blocks. Yep.

VINCE: Whoa! *(They laugh)* Whew!

DOOLEY: I *know. (They laugh)*

VINCE: Poor Dool. *(Pours drink)* Here. Get drunk.

DOOLEY: I am.

VINCE: I tell ya . . . *(Pause)* Drunk? Ladislav? You know "drunk"?

LADISLAV: Drunk. Yes.

VINCE: Schnockered.

LADISLAV: Schnockered.

VINCE: *Good* English. Hammered.

LADISLAV: Hammered.

VINCE: Plowed.

LADISLAV: Hm?

VINCE: Plowed? Like—plow? *(Mimes plowing)*

LADISLAV: Ah! *Plow.*

DOOLEY: Past tense.

LADISLAV: Plowed.

VINCE: Let's get plowed.

LADISLAV: Let's get plowed.

VINCE: What else? Sleep. Going to sleep. Hit the hay?

LADISLAV: Hit—the hay?

DOOLEY: Hit the sack?

VINCE: Turn in.

DOOLEY: Rack up some Z's.

VINCE: What?

DOOLEY: Rack up some Z's? You never heard that?

VINCE: I—*no.* Rack up some Z's?

LADISLAV: Sure.

VINCE: That's for real?

DOOLEY: Yeah.

VINCE: *Okay* . . .

DOOLEY: I think.

VINCE: Or—to go to the bathroom? Bathroom? W.C.?

LADISLAV: Yes! W.C.

VINCE: Yeah. You can say—I have to powder my nose?

DOOLEY: Yeah? Or—

VINCE: I have to see a man about a dog?

DOOLEY: I have to make a deposit?

VINCE: Good one. *(To* LAD) What—whatcha got there?

LADISLAV *(with book)*: *Colloquial English.*

VINCE: Great. *Colloquial English.*

LADISLAV: Bathroom. You say—"I must—visit—my aunt?"
  (Pause)

VINCE: *What?*

LADISLAV: I must—visit my aunt? *(Simultaneously)*

DOOLEY: Never heard *that* one.

VINCE: New one on me.

LADISLAV: Hm.

VINCE: "I must visit my aunt"? What book is that?

LADISLAV: *Colloquial English.*

VINCE: Yeah?

LADISLAV: "I am going to cock my hat"?

VINCE: *What?*

LADISLAV: Yes. See?

VINCE: Let me see that. "I am going to *cock* my *hat.*" I never heard that before in my *life. (To* DOOLEY) Have *you?* (DOOLEY *shrugs)* I don't know, Ladislav. If I were you I'd try to get my money back on this. Somebody made these *up.*

DOOLEY: No, but, "Rack up some Z's," I think that's army.

VINCE: Yeah?

DOOLEY: I think—yeah. That's where I used to hear that.

VINCE: Okay. I don't know. I gotta believe you.

DOOLEY: Yeah.

VINCE: Lad was in the army. Czech army? (LAD *shudders at the memory)*

DOOLEY: Yeah?

VINCE: I first *met* him, he was in uniform.

KATYA: Photograph. *(Goes to get it)*

DOOLEY: Did you hate it?

LADISLAV: Hay-dit?

DOOLEY: Hate? Hate the army?

LADISLAV: Hate! Ah! Yes! Hate! I hated it. Yes.

DOOLEY: Me, too, man. I *hat*ed it.

LADISLAV: Were you—conscript?

DOOLEY: Conscript.

VINCE: Drafted. Yeah.

DOOLEY: Yes! Drafted, yes. Two years.

LADISLAV: Yes. The same.

DOOLEY: *Yeah?* Oh . . .

KATYA *(with framed photo)*: Here he is. Look. *(They look)*

DOOLEY: Yeah . . .

LADISLAV: Very sad man.

DOOLEY: Yep. Me too. But—you were in—which years?

LADISLAV: Which?

DOOLEY: Yeah. Nineteen—?

LADISLAV: Nineteen—sixty-nine, nineteen seventy, nine-teen seventy-one.

DOOLEY: *Yeah?* Same time as me. Went in in sixty-nine, got out in seventy-one.

LADISLAV: Yes?

DOOLEY: *Yes.*

LADISLAV: Did you—go to Vietnam?

DOOLEY: Never did. No. Almost.

LADISLAV: The Czech Army, too.

DOOLEY: Yeah? Really.

LADISLAV: Almost.

DOOLEY: Yeah? Whaddaya *know.*

VINCE: Yeah, but—you understand, there was a slight difference.

DOOLEY: What?

VINCE: Well, if you'd both been sent to Vietnam, you would have fought on—opposite sides. *(Smiles)*

DOOLEY: Is *that right?*

LADISLAV: Yes.

KATYA: Oh, yes.

VINCE: Think about *that.*

DOOLEY: That's—that's pretty interesting.

VINCE: Yep.

LADISLAV: Yes . . . *(Lights change.* SMOCEKOVA's *apartment)*

NARRATOR: At last we found Smocekova, the translator, in her rooms above the square. The creep in the library had told us she was ill, but she didn't look it to me. Smocekova looked like a bulldog in a housecoat, and her temperament suited her looks. Except when she was flirting.

SMOCEKOVA: Let's talk in here. *(With a look)* It's more comfortable. *(They move through a "doorway" to the table, chairs)* Slivovitz?

VINCE: Uh, sure. Thanks.

SMOCEKOVA *(pouring, to* DOOLEY*)*: Do you know *slivovitze?*

VINCE: Plum brandy.

DOOLEY: Ah.

SMOCEKOVA: This is excellent. Made by a colleague of mine, in secret. Far superior to the bowel-rotting swill one finds elsewhere. Drink it. You like it?

DOOLEY: Very good.

SMOCEKOVA *(to* VINCE*)*: You like it?

VINCE: Mm! Yes!

SMOCEKOVA: I'll give you a bottle. The next time you visit. So. When?

VINCE: Oh? *I* don't know.

SMOCEKOVA: Tuesday? Three days from today. Yes?

VINCE: Yes?

SMOCEKOVA: Good. I will prepare dinner for all. Seven p.m. You will be prompt.

VINCE: You bet.

SMOCEKOVA: You, as well.

DOOLEY: Thank you.

VINCE: But we don't want to—I mean, if you're—ill—

SMOCEKOVA: Eh?

VINCE: I mean—are you really—sick?

SMOCEKOVA *(Pause)*: No, not at all. No. But don't tell any Czech. Really. Even my friends don't know about this.

VINCE: What? Are you—what?

SMOCEKOVA: I'm—"biding time." Those idiots at the Strahov Library. Bastards. I had two years before retirement. They wanted to fire me. Luckily, I found a doctor who would say that I was ill, and must remain at home. So. Here I sit.

VINCE: So, you'll stay up here for two years?

SMOCEKOVA: I'll stay up here for one week. Then for another week. Who knows? The idiots at the Strahov may be fired themselves. Replaced by new idiots. Then I would go back. Perhaps.

VINCE: Would you?

SMOCEKOVA: Where else am I to work? I was offered a position with Hradcany Press, but—forbidden, of course. I'm forbidden to translate—Smocek, too. *(To* DOOLEY) My husband. All our works, from thirty years. Forbidden.

VINCE: So what do you do to live?

SMOCEKOVA: What do you think? We translate. Up here. We use fictitious names. Mad, isn't it? The state still requires our services, but we must use pseudonyms. Sometimes, even, they give me my own forbidden translations, to retranslate. It's mad.

VINCE: Do you think things will ever get better here?

SMOCEKOVA: Never.

VINCE: No?

SMOCEKOVA: I don't believe so. Nobody has any guts, anymore. Prime Minister Husak—we all hate him now. That bastard. He went over to them. Signed everything.

VINCE: Well—have you thought of leaving? Could you get out?

SMOCEKOVA: Out of the country? I don't know. Perhaps. But with the situation now, I don't even want to ask about it.

VINCE: And where would you go? I mean—America?

SMOCEKOVA: I would like to, one day, yes.

VINCE: To stay?

SMOCEKOVA: No. I would return here.

VINCE: *Why?* Why not leave for good?

SMOCEKOVA: No. I couldn't. To leave—it would be like leaving a sick child. (VINCE *nods)* Where are you staying, these days?

VINCE: We're staying with Katya; remember her? My interpreter?

SMOCEKOVA: Yes?

DOOLEY: First night, we stayed in the, uh—the Hotel Europa.

SMOCEKOVA: The Europa, yes. It looks like a bordello.

DOOLEY *(laughs):* Yeah. I guess *so.*

SMOCEKOVA *(slyly):* Do you like bordellos?

DOOLEY: *I* don't know.

SMOCEKOVA *(pouring):* Drink. Drink. *(To* VINCE) When you telephoned, you said that you would bring your book.

VINCE *(getting out the galleys):* Here it is.

SMOCEKOVA: Good.

VINCE: Here's your chapter. Can I leave it here?

SMOCEKOVA: If you like. *(Paging through)* Have you seen any of these others?

VINCE: Well, we saw Swoboda, the designer. He showed us around his studio.

DOOLEY: Boy. A*ma*zing stuff, *I* thought. *(They look at him)* I mean. *I,* thought he was just *very good.*

SMOCEKOVA *(shrugs)*: The foremost designer in the world.

DOOLEY: *Well*, I—*(He tries a chuckle)* I'd go along with that. *(He tries another chuckle)*

SMOCEKOVA: The *slivovitze*—you find it poor?

DOOLEY: No! *(Drinks, smiles)*

SMOCEKOVA: What are you studying?

DOOLEY: What?

SMOCEKOVA: In university. You are a student?

DOOLEY: Oh! Yeah. I'm—learning to make—false teeth.

SMOCEKOVA *(to VINCE)*: False *teeth*.

VINCE: Yeah. I told you that.

SMOCEKOVA: I thought you were joking. *(Drinks. To DOOLEY)* Have you ever had a woman?

DOOLEY *(smiles, chokes, clears his throat)*: Hey. *(Tries a chuckle)* A gentleman never tells.

SMOCEKOVA *(to VINCE)*: "A gentleman never tells." You hear that? A good, evasive answer. A charming boy. He will be a charming man, once he gets a piece of ass. *(She produces a pipe, lights up)*

VINCE *(eventually)*: So *any*way . . .

SMOCEKOVA: So. Have you been to see theatre?

VINCE: Couple of things. Last night we went to see a Czech musical version of *Harvey*.

SMOCEKOVA: Why?

VINCE: It was all that was on.

SMOCEKOVA: Stupid.

VINCE: It was. Yes.

SMOCEKOVA: But—you've had successful interviews?

VINCE: Well, it's been hard. I mean, most of the people I talked with seem to be gone, or working someplace else. We spent all today trying to find Petka. You know, the composer?

SMOCEKOVA: Petka? No. You'll never find Petka.

VINCE: One place, they said he was travelling.

SMOCEKOVA: Travelling, yes. He's paying a visit to Switzerland. For the past three years. With his wife, whom he carried out of the country in a suitcase. Travelling.

VINCE: Really?

SMOCEKOVA: Yes.

DOOLEY: In a *suit*case?

SMOCEKOVA: Yes. Who else? Cibulka is dead now, did you know?

VINCE: I heard. I was sorry.

SMOCEKOVA: Yes. Ate himself to death.

VINCE: Oh, yeah?

SMOCEKOVA: Stupid. A stupid way to die. "Here lies a great author and gentle soul—regrettably cut down in the prime of his life by an overfondness for cheese."

VINCE: Hmm.

SMOCEKOVA: Disgusting. Is anyone helping you find these people?

VINCE: Uh, Illinova? At the National Museum?

SMOCEKOVA: Yes?

VINCE: Calling some people for us.

SMOCEKOVA: Illinova. Then you have seen Lozek.

VINCE: No, we're gonna see him tonight. In *Hamlet.*

SMOCEKOVA: Ah, yes. Illinova has always been Lozek's mistress, did you know that?

VINCE: Uh—*no.*

SMOCEKOVA: Everyone knows it. The three of them, can you imagine it? All these years, spending holidays together—Lozek, Illinova and her husband, Illin.

VINCE: I'd never met him.

SMOCEKOVA *(shrugs)*: Not a bad man. Very handsome, for one so old. Straight as a rifle. But of course, a cuckold.

VINCE: Gee, I never knew that about—them.

SMOCEKOVA: You should have asked me. Who else have you seen?

VINCE: Uh, trying to track down Jiri Langer.

SMOCEKOVA: A swine.

VINCE: What? Who?

SMOCEKOVA: Langer. Perhaps he's not a swine. I shouldn't judge him. He's an actor.

VINCE: But—have you heard something?

SMOCEKOVA *(shrugs)*: I know he got into trouble. Something he said. He held his ground, for a time. But then the National Theatre wanted him and he offered to sell his soul—pledge loyalty to the party, and so on. But it was too late. He's forbidden to work here now. He works in the provinces, occasionally in film.

VINCE: What do you—I mean—every, almost everyone I've mentioned, you know something terrible about. I'm almost afraid to—

SMOCEKOVA: These people do terrible things, I hear about them. You ask me and I tell you the truth. Are you complaining?

VINCE: No.

SMOCEKOVA: If you want lies, go outside. You'll have your pick. Pleasant lies, unpleasant, lies about the Russians, the artists, *Praha,* America, me. Free. Gratis. In here with me, you have no such luxury.

VINCE: It must be hard to know who to trust.

SMOCEKOVA: It's not hard. It's easy. Trust no one.

VINCE: No one?

SMOCEKOVA: Two people. Two people I trust, only. One—my husband Smocek—

VINCE: Yeah?

SMOCEKOVA: The other—Frantisek Prchlik.

VINCE: Prchlik?

SMOCEKOVA: Yes. You know his work.

VINCE: What—uh, what does he do?

SMOCEKOVA (*lifting her glass*): He makes this *slivovitze* (*Toasting*) Health. (*Light change.* LAD *and* KATYA's. DOOLEY *sits on "couch" with galleys and photos, matching them and making occasional notations on the backs of the photos.* VINCE *enters, cold)*

DOOLEY: What's cookin'?

VINCE: Nothing. Feeding the goddam pay phone again. I just went through a whole pocketful of *grushkes*, or *schmotkas*, or whatever the goddam hell those things are—

DOOLEY: *Korona.*

VINCE: Yeah, close. Where's Katya?

DOOLEY: In the kitchen.

VINCE (*calling*): Hi, babe!

KATYA (*off*): Yes?

VINCE: Nothing! Hello!

KATYA *(off)*: One moment!

VINCE: It's all right!

DOOLEY: Any luck down there?

VINCE: The National Theatre says they no longer have a number for Langer, you believe that? The *National Theatre*. For Pavlicek, they told me to call the University; then the University told me to call the Ministry of Culture, who advised me that I could probably find Pavlicek someplace called *Narodni Divadlo*. I was in the middle of dialing when I remembered what the *Narodni Divadlo* was.

DOOLEY: What?

VINCE: The National Theatre.

DOOLEY: Geez.

VINCE: Where the fuck *is* he? I named my *son* after him. I wanta have *cof*fee. Ah, well.

DOOLEY: So, what are you gonna do now?

VINCE: Go down, try again. You got any *schmotkas* on you?

DOOLEY: Sure. *(Hands him coins) Korona.*

VINCE: If this doesn't work, I'm gonna hang it up. Go to a nightclub. Drink some Coca-Colas. Can't fuckin' believe it.

KATYA *(entering)*: Are you—well?

VINCE: Oh, I'm all right. How's things here?

KATYA: I'm preparing the pancakes.

VINCE: Oh, *yeah?*

KATYA *(nods)*: From the mixture you brought me.

VINCE: *Okay,* then. Having some *pan*cakes.

KATYA: They may not compare favorably with those of
the true Mother Jemeema, but—

VINCE: Aunt Jemima.

KATYA: Aunt—

VINCE: They'll be fine.

KATYA: But—

VINCE: They'll be just fine.

KATYA: Also—I have no potatoes.

VINCE: Aww, *no.* Pancakes without po*ta*toes? Aww. I
don't know. I don't think Mother Jemeema would approve of that a bit.

KATYA: It's all right? You are joking?

VINCE: Hey. Listen—I can get a potato later. At the nightclub. Coke and a potato. Mmm!

KATYA: You'll go to a nightclub?

VINCE: Sure. You know. I thought maybe I'd run into Pavlicek and Langer there. Maybe they've got an act.

KATYA: You are—too crazy.

VINCE: I'm starting to think so too. *(To* DOOLEY, *who is still working)* What's this?

DOOLEY: Collating a few things. I'm *read*ing some of this.

VINCE: Good. How's the spelling?

DOOLEY: Vince—this is amazing stuff.

VINCE: Yeah, you see?

DOOLEY: What you mean. Yeah.

VINCE *(to* KATYA): You gotten a chance to look at this?

KATYA: I have read—some portions.

VINCE: So? And?

KATYA: I must—finish. But—

VINCE *(seeing a new picture in* DOOLEY'*s hand)*: Hey! There's where we were yesterday. Kafka's place. *(To* KATYA) See? *(Pause.* KATYA *nods)* Good shot, Dool.

DOOLEY: Yeah?

VINCE: And the tobacco store? Oh! 'D you show her your new cigars? Look at these. You got 'em on ya?

DOOLEY: Yeah. *(Producing a box of long, weird cigars)* Here. Vince thought I should buy some Czech cigars. So—

KATYA: Yes?

DOOLEY: I thought these had the most interesting name. *Virzinky?*

KATYA: *Virzinky,* yes. These are—imported.

DOOLEY: Imported?

KATYA: Yes. *Virzinky.* It means—"Virginia."

DOOLEY: "Vir—"? These are imported from Vir*gin*ia?

KATYA: Yes.

DOOLEY: Oh, great.

KATYA: Very expensive.

DOOLEY: *Yeah.* (VINCE *is laughing)* Okay.

VINCE: I'm sorry.

DOOLEY: I'm sure.

VINCE: Really—(LADISLAV *enters, with a proud, carefully rehearsed announcement)* Hiya, Lad.

LADISLAV *(removing coat, etc.)*: Well. *It's*—getting colder. But I hope—that, tomorrow—*it*—may grow warm again. *(He smiles proudly. A beat, then* VINCE *and* DOOLEY *break into applause)*

VINCE: Ya-a-ay! *(Whistles. Smugly,* LAD *exits to the kitchen)* Coming right along, that boy.

KATYA: He is grateful to have you here.

VINCE: Yep. Grateful to *be* here. Well. Be right back. Two more calls. *(At door)* Hey. Sorry about the cigars.

DOOLEY: It's okay.

VINCE: Really. What can I—? You want to sell 'em?

DOOLEY: Get outta here.

VINCE: Okay—*(He is out)*

DOOLEY: Dope.

KATYA: He's having no luck, on the telephone?

DOOLEY: Not much. It's a shame, too. I wanta meet some of these people now. It must have been interesting going around with him on these. Was it?

KATYA: Oh, yes.

DOOLEY: They really opened up to him, didn't they?

KATYA: Hm?

DOOLEY: I mean, these talks seem very—personal.

KATYA: Yes.

DOOLEY: Surprising.

KATYA: Yes. Because they didn't fear him. You see?

DOOLEY: Right.

KATYA: He would seem friendly. Even foolish.

DOOLEY: Yep. That's Vince.

KATYA: So they would talk freely.

DOOLEY: Uh-huh. *(With picture)* Oh, look. Here's you.

KATYA: Oh! In the morning! Oh!

DOOLEY: That's right.

KATYA: Oh! This is not—for the book?

DOOLEY: No!

KATYA: Oh.

DOOLEY: No, no. This is just for me.

KATYA: Ah.

DOOLEY: Some of these.

KATYA: Ah.

DOOLEY: To help me—remember.

KATYA: Yes.

DOOLEY *(another shot)*: You and Lad?

KATYA: Hm.

DOOLEY *(another)*: Vince? Under the clock?

KATYA: Excellent.

DOOLEY: Yeah?

KATYA: Truly. Truly.

DOOLEY: Well, I just—dabble.

KATYA: No. Quite good. Truly.

DOOLEY: You want to see something? *(Producing some drawings)* These are just—

KATYA: Oh! Yours?

DOOLEY: Yeah. Just—couple sketches.

KATYA: You are an artist?

DOOLEY: No. No.

KATYA: Yes. Look.

DOOLEY: I just did these from some of the photos. You know.

KATYA: Just look!

DOOLEY: For the fun of it. I mean, I know they're not really, uh . . .

KATYA: Excellent.

DOOLEY: No, no. I mean, they're not what you'd really call—

KATYA: Excellent.

DOOLEY: No—

KATYA *(insisting)*: They are *just fine.*

DOOLEY: Well—thank you.

KATYA: Yes . . .

DOOLEY: I don't normally, uh . . .

KATYA: Will you become an artist in America?

DOOLEY: Oh, no.

KATYA: No?

DOOLEY: No.

KATYA: Why?

DOOLEY: Oh, I couldn't. It's too—*(Shrugs)*

KATYA: Difficult?

DOOLEY: Well, yeah.

KATYA: In America?

DOOLEY: Oh, yeah.

KATYA: Hm. *(They look at the drawings)* What will you become?

DOOLEY: I'm—*(He stops himself)* I—haven't decided.

KATYA *(holding up a drawing)*: Ah! Such a little boy!

DOOLEY: Yeah. He was one of the—*(Showing her a photo)* Here's the photo. They were all playing kickball the other night, in the Square.

KATYA: Ah. I am enchanted with this little boy.

DOOLEY: Well, then, here. You want this?

KATYA: Oh, no.

DOOLEY: Oh, no, here. I want you to have it.

KATYA: Truly?

DOOLEY: Oh, sure. *(She looks at the picture, laughs)* Katya! I've never heard you laugh.

KATYA *(shaking head)*: I am too enchanted.

DOOLEY *(laughs)*: Ah . . . *(Pause)* Would you fit in a suitcase, do you think?

KATYA: Hm?

DOOLEY: Nothing. *(With another photo)* Look at this. Some people making a movie. This was that same night that—

KATYA *(sees the remaining photo in his hand, takes it, stands)*: Aah!

DOOLEY: Yeah. Oh, yeah.

KATYA: Who is this?

DOOLEY: That's that crazy man, remember? The man off in the alley, in the dark.

KATYA *(in disbelief)*: No.

DOOLEY: Pretty scary, huh?

KATYA: You haven't shown this to Vince?

DOOLEY: Not yet—

KATYA: No. Oh. No, you must not show this to Vince. Ladislav!

DOOLEY: What? What is it? *(Pause. She is staring at the photo)* You know him?

KATYA: It's Pavlicek. Ladislav! *(Pause)*

DOOLEY: What—?

KATYA: It's Pavlicek. *(Blackout. End of act)*

ACT II

NARRATOR *(entering)*: *Any*way.Yeah, hi. So, anyway—that night we showed the picture to Ladislav, and asked him what he thought. Ladislav wasn't much help, never having even seen Pavlicek. Katya still insisted that I not show it to Vince, but I thought I probably would, anyway. Later. I mean, I figured, you know—I'd wait till things got a little better, first. *(As he exits)* Always a mistake. (DOOLEY *is sitting in* ILLINOVA's *office. Coffee, cups on desk)*

VINCE *(entering)*: *Got* him!

DOOLEY *(standing)*: Who?

VINCE: Langer.

DOOLEY: Oh. I thought you meant—

VINCE: No.

DOOLEY: No. But—Jiri Langer? Really?

VINCE *(nods)*: At the TV studio.

DOOLEY: Hey, great.

VINCE: Where's Illinova?

DOOLEY: Be right back, she says.

VINCE *(taking cup)*: *Yeah*. He's so—he sounds so American, I'd forgotten that. I said, "When—will we come—to station?" And he said, "Well, we'll be shooting at about eleven."

DOOLEY: So we're gonna see him?

VINCE *(nods)*: Tomorrow morning, at the State Television Complex; he says, "Just walk in. Try not to speak any English." So we'll take Katya with us. Wait'll you meet this guy. He's a hoot.

DOOLEY: What's he filming?

VINCE: Oh, something, he told me, he's a young Nazi soldier, and he's stranded in the Moscow winter, he's dodging bullets and freezing and dying, and—you know.

DOOLEY: Sounds exciting.

VINCE: Yeah, I said, "Is it good?" He says, "It's a piece of shit. But come anyway."

ILLINOVA *(entering with a large book)*: Hello. Sorry. Did you contact Jiri Langer?

VINCE: I did. Thanks for that number.

ILLINOVA: Yes. Good.

VINCE: Hey, we saw *Hamlet* last night.

ILLINOVA: Yes. Dooley tells me so. And?

VINCE: Well, it made *Harvey* look pretty good.

ILLINOVA: Yes.

VINCE: Lozek was great, though.

DOOLEY: He was.

ILLINOVA *(with a quiet smile)*: Yes. Lozek. Did you speak with him?

VINCE: Just for a minute, after. I said, "You're the best actor here; why aren't you playing Hamlet?" He said, "At my age, I should be playing Yorick." (ILLINOVA *laughs)* So.

ILLINOVA: So you enjoyed Lozek. And Dooley admired the sets.

DOOLEY: I did. Yep.

VINCE: Oh, he told you that?

DOOLEY: Yeah.

VINCE: Yeah, Dooley thinks Swoboda has a lot of promise, as a designer. (DOOLEY *grins, hands in pockets)*

ILLINOVA *(with the book)*: Here. Look.

DOOLEY *(opening it)*: Oh! These are—

ILLINOVA: Swoboda. All his designs.

DOOLEY: My goodness. 1945?

ILLINOVA: Yes.

DOOLEY: Wow.

VINCE: Pretty crafty, old Swobe. (DOOLEY *keeps paging through. To* ILLINOVA) Oh—*(Taking out a pad)* Another couple of names, here, okay? Any word on Vanek?

ILLINOVA: No. I have contacted the Dilia Literary Agency, but, so far, no reply.

VINCE: All right. Who else? Oh! You know who else I'm having trouble finding? You won't believe this. Pavlicek. (DOOLEY *looks up*)

ILLINOVA: Oh. Don't bring Pavlicek into this story.

VINCE: What—story, what do you mean?

ILLINOVA: Pavlicek has had trouble enough, these days.

VINCE: Trouble? You mean—political?

ILLINOVA: Yes.

VINCE: But—so, what? I shouldn't even call him?

ILLINOVA: No. Please.

VINCE: Well—could you talk to him for me?

DOOLEY: Vince—Let's not.

VINCE *(to* ILLINOVA*)*: I just need a little update for the last chapter. See—

ILLINOVA: Please. Vincent. Let Pavlicek enjoy some quiet. *(Pause)*

VINCE: All right.

ILLINOVA: Please.

VINCE: All right. *(Pause)* I promise.

ILLINOVA *(laughs)*: Oh, you don't have to promise. If you tell me you won't do something, I know you won't.

VINCE: If you say not to. But—

ILLINOVA: Dear man. You are so stubborn. Stubborn, stubborn.

VINCE *(forcing a smile)*: Well, I try.

ILLINOVA: Do you never take some rest? Walk around, a little?

VINCE: We do. Every day.

ILLINOVA: Yes?

VINCE: Sure. Dooley'll show you pictures.

ILLINOVA: Good.

VINCE: Sure.

ILLINOVA: And do you see many changes, since the last time you were here?

VINCE: Uh, *yeah.* Lipstick.

ILLINOVA: Lipstick. Yes.

VINCE: Coca-Cola. Blue jeans. Bright clothing.

ILLINOVA: Yes.

VINCE: I don't know if I like it.

ILLINOVA: You don't like it?

VINCE: I don't know. Do you?

ILLINOVA: Why don't you like it?

VINCE: It's too much like—It's too—

ILLINOVA: Too much like America?

VINCE: *Yeah.* Like the *worst* of America. *Plas*tic America.

ILLINOVA: I see, yes. *(A little smile)* And without these things—blue jeans, lipstick—do you think we were a better people?

VINCE: Well, I can't think that—that these things are an improvement.

ILLINOVA *(a shrug)*: Were we better for having only one style of coat to choose from, each winter, do you think? Did that improve our intellect?

VINCE: No. Of course not.

ILLINOVA: So, then—if people want these things and can buy them, why shouldn't they have them?

VINCE: The thing is—all right, I'll tell you, I just can't help feeling that the people here are being bought.

ILLINOVA: "Bought"?

VINCE: *Yeah,* that—all right, you can say there's nothing really wrong with nightclubs and makeup and fancy clothes. But—where's the theatre? What's happened to the artists? I feel like they've been taken away, and that the people have been paid off in—lipstick.

ILLINOVA: No. Believe me, it's not so dramatic.

VINCE: I don't know.

ILLINOVA: No. Perhaps you don't.

VINCE: But—don't you think there's been a change?

ILLINOVA: What sort of change?

VINCE: Just, in people's be*hav*ior. Five years ago, everybody would talk to me. They *want*ed to talk to me. They were—*fear*less. That's why the arts, why the theatre was so good here. Because the people had nothing, and they were *strug*gling. Now they've got *some*thing, but it's—you know, the Kit-Kat Klub.

ILLINOVA: So—you would rather we were more poor, more unhappy, so that our arts will be more interesting for you?

VINCE: Well, don't put it that way, but—I mean, it is frustrating. To see.

ILLINOVA: Yes. *(Kindly)* Ah. It's such a pity. One moment you decide it might be pleasant to fly to Czechoslovakia. Your publisher gives you money, and you go. There is no one to stop you. You are looking forward to seeing again the Czech people creating art from ashes. But how sad for you—there are fewer ashes than before.

VINCE: Shit.

ILLINOVA *(lightly)*: We are no longer so—picturesque.

VINCE: I'm not—

ILLINOVA: More coffee?

VINCE: Thank you. *(She pours coffee)* I'm not begrudging anybody their prosperity, but you've gotta ask, at what price? I mean, if the artists are gone and the reason is that—that—I mean, surely it's wrong for artists to be forbidden to work because of their political beliefs.

ILLINOVA: Yes. But . . . you had a similar period in America, did you not? *(A long pause)*

VINCE: I guess we did.

ILLINOVA: Yes?

VINCE: But that doesn't mean it's right.

ILLINOVA: No, but, you see, such things happen even in the most enlightened nations. Cream? *(Blackout. Lights up on an isolated area, C. Overturned tables, chairs.* JIRI LANGER—*Actor "A"—in a Nazi helmet, stumbles in, shouting desperately into a walkie-talkie)*

LANGER: Hallo! Hallo! *Sleeshesh m'nyeh? Yeh too nyegdo? Ya sem poslyednyi. Ya sem poslyednyi od Hitler-oveekh tsupermanoo na Roosky zemi. (He collapses, bumps his head, touches the bump, inspects his fingers for blood)* Hallo . . . hallo . . . *(He falls. He does not rise. Lights up to full, to show* KATYA, VINCE, *and* DOOLEY *seated in a row at the side of the stage.* LANGER *rises, exits disgustedly)*

KATYA: They will do it again.

VINCE *(to* DOOLEY): He's good, huh?

DOOLEY: Yeah.

VINCE: What was he saying, Katya?

KATYA *(with her notation pad)*: He said—"Can anyone hear me? Is anyone there? If anyone is there, then know—that I am the last. The last of Hitler's supermen alive on Russian soil. Our blood was not hot enough to brave a Moscow winter."

VINCE: Uh-huh.

LANGER *(entering as before)*: Hallo! Hallo! *Sleeshesh m'nyeh? Yeh too nyegdo? Ya sem poslyednyi. Ya sem poslyednyi od Hitleroveekh tsupermanoo na Roosky zemi. (Collapses, bumps head, touches bump, inspects fingers)* Hallo . . . hallo . . . *(He falls, lies still, breaks character, rises, exits)*

KATYA: They are finished. We should go to the commissary.

VINCE: Right. *(As they walk)* But he's okay, huh? Okay actor?

DOOLEY: Yeah.

VINCE: Except for maybe that part where he bumped his head and felt it with his finger, that was a little—

DOOLEY: Yeah.

VINCE: But still—

DOOLEY: Oh, yeah. No. He's good.

KATYA: We will meet Langer at the bar. *(They sit)*

VINCE *(opening attaché)*: Give him his chapter, here. *(To* DOOLEY) Let's get his picture, if we can.

DOOLEY: Okay.

VINCE *(to* KATYA): Have you finished this yet?

KATYA: Hm?

VINCE: The book. Have you read it all, yet?

KATYA: Yes.

VINCE: So?

KATYA: I have given it to Lad, to read.

VINCE: Okay. Well, what did *you* think?

KATYA *(grateful to see* LANGER): Jiri Langer. Here he is. *("A" enters as* LANGER)

LANGER: Ah! Welcome! Yes.

VINCE: Jiri. Good to see you. You remember Katya.

LANGER: Yes? Sure?

VINCE: And Bob Dooley?

LANGER: How are you doing?

DOOLEY: Fine.

LANGER: Fine. Good.

VINCE: We enjoyed the filming. You looked good.

DOOLEY: Yeah.

LANGER: It was a piece of shit. But thanks. *(To* KATYA, *in Czech)* Promeeneh. [I'm sorry.]

KATYA *(in Czech)*: *Neh, neh. Doyeh yehno obreebehneh slovo.* [Don't be. It's his favorite word.]

LANGER *(smiles. To* VINCE): She says, "Don't apologize. Shit is his favorite word." *(In Czech, to an offstage barkeep)* Vodka, *proseem. Flashkoo. (In English)* Shit is all I do now. I'm a specialist.

VINCE: Why do you feel that?

LANGER: It's true. There's money in it, don't worry about that.

VINCE: Yeah?

LANGER: Sure. Yeah. I'm—healthy and wealthy. Can I help it if the stuff they give me to act is—? *(He gestures)*

VINCE: Yeah.

LANGER *(reaching offstage for the bottle and glasses. In Czech)*: *Dyekooyoo.* [Thanks.] *(In English, pouring)* Vodka. This is on me.

VINCE: Thanks.

DOOLEY: Thank you. (KATYA *nods thanks)*

LANGER: We'll drink to art, yes?

VINCE & DOOLEY: To art.

LANGER: Later we'll drink to television.

VINCE: All right. *(They laugh)* So you do a lot of TV now.

LANGER: A lot of TV. Yeah. *(He smiles, waves at someone offstage)* We should keep our voices down. That woman in the white coat is no good.

VINCE: I thought she was watching us.

LANGER *(nods)*: She drives a Tatra, that beauty. You don't get a Tatra by cleaning tables. Do you know what I mean?

VINCE: Un-huh.

LANGER *(with bottle)*: Here. Finish that. *(Pours)*

VINCE: Eleven forty-five in the morning. *(Drinks.* DOOLEY *drinks too)* This is quite a place, though.

LANGER: The TV complex, yes. It's bigger every day. See those guys at that table? Construction workers. Always, always building.

VINCE: They look like a pretty rough bunch.

LANGER: No, they're good guys. Good types. We buy drinks for each other. *(He waves)* Hallo!

VINCE: But you're—successful?

LANGER: Sure, yeah. I'm lucky. Many actors can't work at all. So I'm—very lucky.

VINCE: You happy?

LANGER: Sure. Why not? Yeah.

VINCE: You ever do any stage work these days?

LANGER: Sometimes. Not often. Last year I played Dr. Faustus in the town of Kladno.

VINCE: Kladno? Where's that?

LANGER: No one knows. (VINCE *laughs)*

VINCE: But I'm sure they knew *you,* though.

LANGER: From TV. Sure. Guys were always coming up to me, saying, "My wife's in love with ya. Ya gotta have a drink with me."

VINCE: You ever work with Zebrova anymore?

LANGER: No.

VINCE: Not at all?

LANGER: No.

VINCE: What is she doing now?

LANGER: I—I don't know. Zebrova and I—we're no longer in touch.

VINCE: No? You two were such a great acting team.

LANGER: Yes. Thanks. But—no. There's no reason. I don't know what reason.

VINCE: Did she—break it up?

LANGER: Break it up?

VINCE: Did she—go away? From you?

LANGER: No. I don't think so. You could say—our lives were guided into separate directions. You see?

VINCE: I think.

LANGER: You're not drinking.

VINCE: I'm drinking. *(Drinks)*

LANGER: Here. *(Pours)*

VINCE: I was hoping you'd be in something at the National.

LANGER: No. The National manages pretty well, without me.

VINCE: They *don't*, though. They're doing *lousy*.

LANGER *(with a sad smile)*: Yes. They are somewhat lousy these days, aren't they?

VINCE: *Yeah.* So why don't you work for them? Help them out?

LANGER: You're asking this to the wrong guy, my friend.

VINCE: You just—maybe I shouldn't be asking about this.

LANGER: You can ask. But don't expect answers. I don't know the answers for you.

VINCE: Yeah.

LANGER: One never knows the reasons for these things, you see? One day, you're working, you're—you've achieved some fame, you're—free to pick and choose. Everything's good. The next day, you're restricted. You no longer have choices. Your name is everywhere on some government list. "Why?" you ask. But you never know why. Not really. A letter has come down from somewhere. Someone has decided that your work must be—supervised. "Who has decided this?" You don't know. No one tells you. And so—who can you fight? Who can you plead with? No one. This Mister No-one, who has taken a few minutes from his day to send down this letter to change your life. "What have I said? What have I done, to deserve this?" Something, surely. Some talk, or something you've done, has been interpreted to mean—something. But you don't even know what that is. So if you're absolutely careful, you don't do or say *any*thing from then on. You become a robot. Yes?

VINCE: Mm-hm. And—has that happened to you? Have you become a robot?

LANGER: No. Not really. But—I have a few mechanical parts. More than I would like.

VINCE: Jiri—why don't you come to the States?

LANGER *(shrugs)*: It's not so easy, you know. You always leave someone behind—family, friends. Someone who can be made to suffer in your absence.

VINCE: Yeah.

LANGER: But—there may be—possibilities. We'll see about it.

VINCE: Uh-huh. Let me know if—you know.

LANGER: Yes. I know. Thanks.

VINCE: I wish I knew enough to make—suggestions.

LANGER: No. You're right to suggest nothing. No one can know, really, what it is to be a Czech. *(To* KATYA) How should I explain? *(To* VINCE) You may think that you view one of our problems in the same way that we view it, but you don't, really. You can't. Simply because you're not a Czech. Do you see?

VINCE: I guess.

KATYA: Yes. It's true.

LANGER: Everyone is always offering solutions to us—great, simple solutions, to everything. Then they are surprised when we become—offended?

KATYA: Offended. Yes.

LANGER: Yes. In some sense.

VINCE: Yeah.

LANGER *(pouring)*: One more. Then I must go back to making shit.

VINCE: I'm sorry you have to do this.

LANGER: It's—the times, that's all. When the spirit of rebellion is high, when the pressure is on, drama becomes much better.

VINCE: What a shame, though. Remembering how great the theatre was five years ago, and now knowing it's—lost.

LANGER: It isn't lost. Wait another five years. (VINCE *nods.* LANGER *rises. To* DOOLEY) Good to meet you.

DOOLEY: Thanks.

LANGER: Katya?

KATYA: Goodbye.

LANGER: Goodbye.

VINCE: I'll call you.

LANGER: Good. Goodbye! Good luck!

VINCE: So long!

LANGER: So long! Yes. *(He exits. They sit a few moments)*

VINCE: Oh, boy . . .

DOOLEY: Are we drunk?

VINCE: I don't know. Yeah.

DOOLEY: Schnockered? (VINCE *smiles a little)* Plowed?

VINCE *(nodding)*: Hm.

DOOLEY: What is it?

VINCE: *Lan*ger. He seemed so—you should have seen him before. He was a mati*nee* idol. He was Paul *New*man. You know?

DOOLEY: Yeah?

VINCE: Now he seems so—*sad.* I don't know. I hate it. You should have seen him with Zebrova. His partner. Beautiful. *(To* KATYA) You saw them together.

KATYA: Many times.

VINCE: They'd play love scenes. And in the middle of nothing, he'd lift her onto his shoulder, and they'd play out the scene like that—walking around. Just lift her right up. Easy as pie. Light filtering down.

DOOLEY: Hm.

VINCE: Sounds ridiculous, but God, it worked. Tore your fuckin' heart out. And now she's where? Some factory, somewhere? Putting the caps on bottles of *Coke?* Shit. I don't know. I don't mean to—.

DOOLEY: No. It's . . .

CONSTRUCTION WORKER *(offstage)*: Hallo!

KATYA: Someone is coming.

DOOLEY *(waving)*: One of the construction guys.

KATYA: Yes.

DOOLEY: You want to go? (VINCE *shrugs. "A" enters as a jolly, soused worker)*

CONSTRUCTION WORKER: *Room pro Langrovee voo kamaradyi!*

KATYA: He wants to buy rum for all of Langer's friends.

DOOLEY *(laughing)*: Ah! No!

CONSTRUCTION WORKER: *Ano! (He signals the bartender)*

DOOLEY: No! No!

KATYA: It's too late. *("A," having gotten bottle, pours, speaking)*

DOOLEY: Oh, boy. Sorry.

CONSTRUCTION WORKER: *Nyay sem komoneesta ee sem yen yerneek. Ala veem veets nesh moyshef.*

KATYA: He says, "I am not a Communist. I am only a worker. Yet my fellow workers and I are more clever than the leader of the entire enterprise." (DOOLEY *toasts him halfheartedly. He beams)*

DOOLEY *(offering one)*: Cigarette? *(The worker gestures, "No thanks." DOOLEY nods, pockets them again. They sit. The worker smiles. Trying again, offering box)* Cigar?

CONSTRUCTION WORKER *(in awe, delightedly taking one)*: *Virzinky!*

DOOLEY: That's right. *(He can't help smiling at* KATYA *and* VINCE. *The worker lights up happily)*

VINCE *(referring to the bus person)*: Look at her over there. Not being too obvious, is she? That's gotta be the cleanest table in town, by now.

DOOLEY *(looking too)*: Hm. *(Pause)*

VINCE: I think maybe it's time to get on the plane.

DOOLEY: You think?

VINCE: I don't know. Maybe we're pressing our luck.

DOOLEY: Yeah?

VINCE: I don't know.

CONSTRUCTION WORKER: John, George, Paul, Ringo! Hanh? *(Pause)* Hanh? *(Pause)* Elvis Presley?

VINCE *(ignoring the worker)*: I mean—I think we've seen everybody they're gonna let us see. There's no theatre really. So—maybe our chapter's written. Maybe it's time to go.

DOOLEY: Okay.

VINCE: I really think.

DOOLEY: Okay. *(Pause)*

CONSTRUCTION WORKER: Perry Como? *(Light change.* LAD *and* KATYA's. *"A" steps forward)*

NARRATOR: A silent taxi homeward through the Square. Signs and storefronts passing by, suddenly familiar. Odd. Late that night—coffee in the kitchen with Lad and Katya. I was writing postcards. It was a long time before I realized what was being talked about.

VINCE: But he *said* these things. Y'know? The man *said* these things.

KATYA: To you.

VINCE: To me, yes. But not—off the record.

KATYA: "Off the record"?

VINCE: Not—he knew I was working on a book. Right? You were there. The tape recorder was on? He knew whatever he said might end up in print. He didn't say, "Don't print."

KATYA: Still. *(Pause)*

VINCE: What else—what should I have done?

KATYA: Sometimes . . . I think, a friendly question is more dangerous than a question—not friendly. Do you understand? (VINCE *shrugs)* As you have said, the tape recorder was running, and he knew that you might write whatever he might say. But—because you speak to him as a friend—in the manner of a friend—in a little time the tape recorder vanishes, in some sense.

VINCE: Well . . . *Yeah.* I *want*ed the tape recorder to vanish. In a way. I wanted him to be comfortable.

KATYA: Yes?

VINCE: *Yes.* So that he would—speak honestly. That's— *(He makes a frustrated gesture)* What do I mean? If—if he speaks not honestly, but if he speaks only officially, and I write it down, then that part of the book becomes —official—propaganda. You see what I mean? I don't want that. *(Pause)*

LADISLAV: It's a difficult question.

KATYA: If—if you should approach him as a friend . . .

VINCE: Yes.

KATYA: He accepts your friendship. He speaks into your recorder, he speaks freely. Honestly. But this does not mean, as you believe, that whatever he says may be printed. It means only that he has—transferred—the role of censor, from himself to you. It's a gift, for his friend.

VINCE: Okay. I can buy that. So you think that I've—betrayed his trust?

KATYA: It's not so strong. But—perhaps you are not the best censor for him. Because, as Langer said, only because you're not a Czech. You understand?

VINCE: I don't know the rules. [. . . is what you're saying.]

KATYA: Perhaps you don't know the risks. All of them.

VINCE: All right, listen, if that's what you think, let's call him up. Let's read him this stuff. He can be censor.

KATYA: It's impossible. You know that it's impossible.

VINCE: It's not impossible. You just call him up.

KATYA: It's not impossible, no. It's a risk.

VINCE: So what should I do? You want to be censor? You be censor.

KATYA: No . . .

VINCE: Really, no, that would be—swell. You tell me what —what I should leave out.

KATYA *(studies the page of manuscript)*: It's—impossible.

VINCE: Why? What's impossible?

KATYA: It's—political. Every sentence he says may be seen as political.

VINCE: Well—did he think I was going to quote him about his wife and kids? I'm writing about theatre. I'm not trying to write about politics. But it just so happens that the theatre here *is* politics.

LADISLAV: Yes. Exactly.

KATYA: Yes.

VINCE: So—what can I do? Change his name? I can't change his name. I'd have to change his whole history, and that's—hell. My other choice is to leave him out, right? Leave him out of the book. I hate that. *(Long silence.* LADISLAV *and* KATYA *are looking through the manuscript)* All right, let me—I want to think about this. All right, what else? *(Pause)*

KATYA: Your introduction. It's by Pavel Tigrid.

VINCE: Yeah?

KATYA *(shaking her head. Quietly)*: Pavel Tigrid is a great enemy of our country.

VINCE: Well—I didn't know that, okay? But—*still.* It's only a description of the city. I mean, it's not even o*pin*ion, it's just—it's background.

KATYA: To the authorities, Tigrid's name alone would make the rest—suspect.

VINCE: That's their problem. I mean, I hate to say that, but we can't—we can't make it our objective to please the authorities. Can we? Or do we know they'll read it, even? It's coming out in Indiana, fifteen hundred copies, you think anyone here is even going to see it?

KATYA: Yes.

VINCE: Really?

KATYA: Yes.

LADISLAV: Oh, yes.

KATYA: They will read it. Any book about Czechoslovakia. It would be in the hands of officials here within a few days.

LADISLAV: Yes.

VINCE: Really. That's amazing.

LADISLAV: Yes.

VINCE: All right. Anyway. I don't know what to say about the introduction. I like it. I really like it. When you say "suspect," you mean, do you mean Tigrid's name in the book would make *me* suspect? Because I don't care about that. Or do you mean, make the others in the book suspect?

KATYA: All. Everyone.

VINCE: Everyone. That's what I thought. Well. What can I do? I could paraphrase, I suppose. Change his writing. Leave his name off. *(To* DOOLEY) Do a little plagiarism, *hey,* long as the officials are happy, y'know? Fuck. What I should do is leave the book exactly as it is, and dedicate it to that babe that was watching in the commissary. Fix her wagon. *(To* LAD *and* KATYA, *who are once more looking through the manuscript)* Okay. Let's get through this. So, we've got Marek and Tigrid. Someone else? Anything else we should look at? *(Pause)* Anything? *(A long pause)*

KATYA *(looking at the manuscript. Quietly)*: Many things.

VINCE: "Many things." Okay. Now's the time to tell me.

KATYA: Vanek.

VINCE: Yeah?

KATYA: This is from his play. *Leestek.* "The Ticket."

VINCE: "The Ticket," yeah? *(She shrugs)* I know, it's an anti-establishment play, right? But so what? I mean, it's *fa*mous. It's part of your history. It's *pub*lished.

KATYA: I think, no longer published.

VINCE: Great. So the book could be bad for Vanek, too, you think?

KATYA: I think—it is impossible to predict—but it *could* create trouble for many of these people you write about.

VINCE: "Many" of them?

KATYA: Yes. Possibly. Even those who do not—speak—strongly, may be implicated merely because they appear with those who do.

VINCE: Well, see, here's my problem. You're not leaving me a lot of choices, here. You're saying, one thing I can do is remove everything anybody said or wrote that was anti-authority. Which leaves us with half a book. Maybe. Or, I can change people's names. But they'd still be recognized, right? So I'd have to change their histories, too. Their careers. Which leaves us with what? A big lie. The book was supposed to *be* a history, for cryin' out loud. If we have to be as careful as you're saying, then we might as well not publish it at *all.* Or is that what you're saying? *(Silence)* Is that what you're saying? *(Silence)* Awwww . . . *(Silence)* I don't believe this.

LADISLAV: It is hard to know—what I would do—in your place.

VINCE: You really—you both think—I can't even say it. Katya, you worked with me a year on this. Are you really suggesting what I think you're suggesting?

KATYA: I'm only telling you my beliefs.

VINCE: I know, but—yeah. You've told me your beliefs and now it's my decision, right? Great. So your beliefs are that all these people's heads are on the chopping block waiting for my book to come out. But, *my* decision, right? Wonderful.

KATYA: You are angry?

VINCE: I'm not—yeah, I'm angry. I'm angry. What the hell.

KATYA: Perhaps—it was the wrong time for us to speak.

VINCE: No. No, it wasn't, it was the right time for you to speak. And I'm not angry with you, really, I'm just in a —bad—[position]. I mean—the thing is, I have to believe you. You know? If you tell me there's a danger to these people, how can I say, "No, there isn't"? I can't. So—I don't know how to ask you this, but—I've got to ask you. And you have to be completely honest. Is it *pos*sible, do you think . . . is it *pos*sible that you—that you are more afraid than is necessary? *(Pause)*

KATYA: Yes. We are more afraid than is necessary.

VINCE: Yes?

KATYA: Yes. Those who are less afraid than is necessary are no longer here.

VINCE: Yeah. *(Silence.* VINCE *looks at* DOOLEY. *Smiles brightly) Well. (Exhales audibly, looking away from them)*

LADISLAV: It is a very sad question. *(Silence)* There is a Russian saying—"The morning is more clever than the night." So—we can talk about it in the morning.

VINCE: There is an American saying—"Ohhhhhh . . . shit." *(Light change.* SMOCEKOVA's. VINCE *and* DOOLEY, *with suitcases, approach her "door")*

DOOLEY *(knocks)*: Hello? *(Knocks)* Smocekova? She wouldn't have gone anywhere. *(They look around)*

VINCE: You know something I've always wanted to do? Drive up to one of those phone stores. You know? Places that sell those cute phones? Blast it with a bazooka. Then go for coffee.

DOOLEY: Yeah? *(Knocks.* SMOCEKOVA *answers the "door")*

SMOCEKOVA: You're late.

VINCE: We're late. I know.

SMOCEKOVA: Sit. Eat some ruined dinner.

VINCE *(as they go to the table)*: I'm really sorry.

SMOCEKOVA: It's your loss. Twenty minutes ago, this was the best meal in *Praha.* Now it's for the pigs.

VINCE: I'm sorry.

SMOCEKOVA: Eat. *(Pouring)* Becherovka?

DOOLEY: Thank you.

SMOCEKOVA: You?

VINCE: Yes. I'm really sorry.

SMOCEKOVA: Eat.

DOOLEY *(eating)*: This is really good. Dumplings, or something.

SMOCEKOVA: Yes, it's delicious, when the guests arrive on time.

VINCE: I'm not gonna get out of this, am I?

SMOCEKOVA: Why should you? You're late. Running all over town with that book of yours.

VINCE: That's not it.

SMOCEKOVA: Hah!

VINCE: No. In fact—with the book. In fact—I may not publish it now.

SMOCEKOVA: Why not?

VINCE: It's just that some people think it might hurt some people. Cause them trouble.

SMOCEKOVA: Who suggests this?

VINCE: Oh, a couple of friends.

SMOCEKOVA: Friends! What friends? They are sheep, lacking entrails. Go ahead and publish your book. That's my advice.

VINCE: I really don't know if I can.

SMOCEKOVA: Listen to me. Is this a story that must be told?

VINCE: I thought it was.

SMOCEKOVA: And who else is there to tell it, do you think? Someone here?

VINCE: I don't know.

SMOCEKOVA: No. No one here can tell it. And soon it will be forgotten. Is that what you want?

VINCE: No.

SMOCEKOVA: Well, then.

VINCE: But—if it can possibly hurt people—.

SMOCEKOVA: Listen to me. Whatever anyone says in your book, they have already said elsewhere. Their statements are in some secret file somewhere—statements much more damaging than anything in your book.

VINCE: You think?

SMOCEKOVA: I know it. Eat. The secret police are so stupid, anyway. They won't care about this little book.

VINCE: God, I want to believe that.

SMOCEKOVA: Believe it. Go ahead, publish it.

VINCE: God. I could never tell Katya.

SMOCEKOVA: Publish it. Believe me, no one here will give a damn.

VINCE: I'd have to be so sure of that.

SMOCEKOVA: And think of those people one hundred years from now who may need this book. Have you thought of them?

VINCE: Yes. I have. I do. Well—then—maybe I should.

SMOCEKOVA: Yes, you must, that's all. Eat.

VINCE *(eating idly)*: Maybe I will. Hm. *(Pause, as they eat)*

SMOCEKOVA: Besides, even if this book were to cause anyone to suffer, most would do so gladly for the sake of the truth.

VINCE: Oh, God.

SMOCEKOVA: What.

VINCE: No. See, I can't play with people's lives.

SMOCEKOVA: It's a risk anyone here would take.

VINCE: Anyone *here*.

SMOCEKOVA: Yes.

VINCE: I know. But *I can't*.

SMOCEKOVA: Why not?

VINCE: Because—just because—

DOOLEY: Because he's not a Czech.

VINCE *(looks at DOOLEY, then back at SMOCEKOVA)*: Yeah. *(Pause)*

SMOCEKOVA: It doesn't matter. Do it.

VINCE *(decided)*: No. *(She growls)* No. I have a real problem thinking that way.

SMOCEKOVA: "A real problem"! Hah! I wish I had your problems. Eat! Eat! *(Light change. The "scaffold" again, evening.* VINCE *and* DOOLEY, *with suitcases, enter, stop —looking toward the Square)*

DOOLEY: Wow. So *clear* tonight, look. *(No response from* VINCE) Wait a second. *(He climbs the scaffold, camera in hand)*

VINCE: Trying to get us arrested?

DOOLEY: I'll be all right.

VINCE: Yeah? *(Climbs up beside him.* DOOLEY *takes a shot or two, then they sit watching for a moment)* Hm. *(Shakes head)* Wenceslas Square.

DOOLEY: Yep.

VINCE: Shit.

DOOLEY: I know. I'm sorry.

VINCE: Yeah.

DOOLEY: Anything I can do?

VINCE: Nah. You know. Or, you know what? You know what you can do?

DOOLEY: What.

VINCE *(trying to joke)*: When we get back, could you, uh— sometime, could you take my kids around, and—you know, take 'em around Cementville? Show 'em its finer points?

DOOLEY: Sure.

VINCE: I guess they're gonna have to learn to like it.

DOOLEY: No problem.

VINCE: Shit.

DOOLEY: I know.

VINCE *(brightly)*: So! Well! Hey! Let's see, here. We haven't seen any theatre, I've lost most of my friends, and I'm not publishing the book. We've accomplished a hell of a lot, this trip. *(They laugh a little)* Sorry about the big photographer job.

DOOLEY: It doesn't matter.

VINCE: No, well—

DOOLEY: It doesn't. To me, this has been—it's meant a lot.

VINCE: *Really?*

DOOLEY: Yes. *(Pause)*

VINCE: How? I mean, how? I think I really need to know how.

DOOLEY *(wishing he had a better answer)*: . . . I'm not sure, yet.

VINCE: Yeah.

DOOLEY: But something. But something.

VINCE: Yeah, okay. Well, good. I just—Would you tell somebody about this, someday? Cause that's the *thing*, really. Cause now nobody's gonna *know* about all this.

So if you could just tell somebody. I mean—would you do that?

DOOLEY *(the speech of his life)*: Okay. *(Long pause. They are looking around.* VINCE *checks his watch)*

VINCE: Well—Illinova's waiting up. Let's hit it. Set? *(They pick up their suitcases, start off)* We miss this plane tonight, we're gonna be stuck here till St. Swithin's— *(Suddenly "A," as the* MADMAN *from Act I, appears from the shadows)*

MADMAN: *Anglitsky . . . ! (He grabs* VINCE's *coat)*

DOOLEY *(stepping back startled)*: Ah.

MADMAN: Here! Yes! Do you know me, English??

VINCE: OK. Let go.

MADMAN: Once—

VINCE: Stop it!

MADMAN: Once I was many animals!!

VINCE: *Stop* it!!

MADMAN *(recognizing him)*: Aah! *(He stops)*

VINCE: Goddammit.

MADMAN *(perhaps in Czech)*: It's you. My God, it's you.

DOOLEY: Vince—

MADMAN *(grabbing* VINCE *again. Again, perhaps in Czech)*: You! Look! Look at me!

VINCE: Hey—taxi.

MADMAN: Look at me.

VINCE: Get out of here.

MADMAN: Once I was many animals!

VINCE *(pushing him off)*: Get the fuck *out* of here.

MADMAN: But no more!

VINCE *(spotting one)*: Taxi!

MADMAN: Have you slept with the beautiful stranger?

VINCE *(whistle)*: Hey!

MADMAN: Have you become the food?

VINCE *(to* DOOLEY): Here we go. C'mon. *(He pulls at* DOOLEY)

MADMAN: Once I was many animals but—No more.

VINCE: Dooley? (DOOLEY *follows him toward taxi)*

MADMAN: No. No. My eyes are white. All white eyes. (DOOLEY, *at exit, is still watching him)* My animals are dead. *(Blackout. Lights up instantly on* ILLINOVA'*s.* VINCE *and* DOOLEY *enter with suitcases)*

VINCE: Illinova? Door was open. Well—*(They put down suitcases)*

DOOLEY: But—you're positive.

VINCE: What? Sure. You kidding?

DOOLEY: I—

VINCE: What is this?

DOOLEY: He just—looked like he'd recognized you.

VINCE: Right, yeah. Go to New York, sometime. You'll get recognized too.

DOOLEY: All right. Vince. *(With photo)* Look.

VINCE *(after a moment)*: Same guy.

DOOLEY: Yeah?

VINCE: This was that guy the other night? That—?

DOOLEY: *Yeah.*

VINCE: Whaddaya know.

DOOLEY: So, what do you think?

VINCE: What? I think—uh, it's great. We share the same lunatic. Great.

DOOLEY: Okay.

VINCE: *What.*

DOOLEY *(putting away picture)*: Okay.

VINCE: What was I supposed to say?

ILLINOVA *(entering with two books)*: Vincent?

VINCE: There she is.

ILLINOVA: Ah! I was afraid to have missed you.

VINCE: Well, we are sort of on our way, here. We just wanted to say thanks, again, and goodbye, and—

ILLINOVA: Goodbye, Vincent. Good luck to you.

VINCE: Thanks. I, uh—And, I wanted to tell you—I've been thinking—I don't think I'm going to publish the book.

ILLINOVA: Yes. That's good.

VINCE: Yes? Good not to publish?

ILLINOVA: Yes. That's just what you should do with that book. It's not—necessary.

VINCE: Well, I'm glad you—approve.

ILLINOVA: You have enjoyed your stay, I hope.

VINCE: Sure.

ILLINOVA: I, too, Vincent. You make one feel a child again. That is your great talent.

VINCE: Well—that's good. I was afraid I—American expression—I was afraid I had given you some new grey hairs.

ILLINOVA *(laughs)*: No! *(Laughs)* No. Look. The same number as when you arrived.

VINCE: Good. *(Rising)* Well.

DOOLEY: Goodbye. Thanks.

ILLINOVA: One moment. I have something for you. *(Gives* DOOLEY *a book)* Dooley?

DOOLEY *(looking at it)*: Oh . . .

VINCE: What is it?

DOOLEY: It's the Swoboda book.

VINCE: Yeah.

ILLINOVA: Yes.

DOOLEY: Illinova—this is your copy.

ILLINOVA: No. It's for you.

DOOLEY: Oh. Thank you.

ILLINOVA *(handing* VINCE *the other book)*: And this—photographs of old *Praha.*

VINCE: Yes. Thank you.

DOOLEY *(having found a snapshot in his book)*: Uh, you want this, don't you? It was inside the cover, here.

ILLINOVA *(taking the snapshot gently)*: Oh, yes. Yes. I will keep this. Look. *(They all gather round the picture)* Our forest cabin. Where we holiday each autumn.

VINCE *(looking at it)*: Look at that.

DOOLEY: Beautiful place.

VINCE: Look at those—birches? Birch trees?

ILLINOVA: Birch trees. Yes.

DOOLEY: So *tall.*

ILLINOVA: Yes. It is, very beautiful there. And, silent.

VINCE: And that's you.

ILLINOVA: Me. Yes. And my husband.

VINCE: This? This is your husband.

ILLINOVA: And Lozek.

VINCE: Lozek, yes.

DOOLEY: Oh, yeah.

ILLINOVA: Yes. *(Pause)*

VINCE *(still looking at the photo)*: You seem happy.

ILLINOVA: Yes. *(They look at the photo for a while)* We are all happy, these days. *(They freeze, in the light. After a moment, "A" enters, and speaks quietly toward* VINCE*)*

NARRATOR: Vince? *(Pause)* This is for you. Thanks. *(To the audience)* Good night. *(He exits. Blackout. End of play)*

PRONUNCIATIONS

WORDS

America—ah-MEH-ree-kah
Anglichanyi—AHNG-glee-chahn-yee
Anglitsky—AHNG-gleet-skee
Becherovka—BEX-eh-rohf-kah (X-uvular fricative, as in German "ach," Scottish "loch")
Cibulka—TSEE-bool-kah
Cinohernyi Klub—CHEE-noh-hair-nyee KLOOP
Daneshova, Katya—DAH-neh-shoh-vah, KAH-tyah
Dilia—DEEL-yah
Dubcek—DOOP-check
Dr. Faust—Dohk-tohr FOWST
Europa Hotel—EHV-roh-pah
Gratis—GRAH-tees
Hallo—HAH-loh
Hamlet—HAHM-leht
Hradcany—HRAHT-chah-nee
Illin—EE-lyeen
Illinova—EE-lyee-noh-vah
Kafka—KAHF-kah
Kladno—KLAHD-hoh
Koruna—KOH-roo-nah
Ladislav—LAH-dyee-slahf
Langer, Jiri—LAHNG-gair, YEE-ree
Lozek—LOH-zehk
Marek—MAH-rehk
Narodni Divadlo—NAH-rohd-nyee DYEE-vahd-loh
Palach, Jan—PAH-lahx, YAHN (X-uvular fricative, as in German "ach," Scottish "loch")
Pavlicek, Mikulas—PAHV-lee-chehk, MEE-koo-lahsh
Petka—PEHTY-kah
Praha—PRAH-hah
Prchlik, Frantisek—PRX-leek, FRAHN-tee-shehk
Robot—ROH-boht
Saint Swithin—Saynt SWITH-in (voiced TH as in *the*)
Sarah—SAH-rah

Semafor—SEH-mah-fohr
Skoda—SHKOH-dah
Slivovitze—SLEE-voh-veet-seh
Smocek—SMOH-chehk
Smocekova—SMOCH-koh-vah
Strahov—STRAH-hohf
Tatra—TAH-trah
Leestek—LEE-stehk (Don't say the word "ten.")
Tigrid, Pavel—TEE-greed, PAH-vehl
Vanek—VAH-nyehk
Vietnam—VEE-eht-nahm
Virzinky—VEER-zheeng-kee
Zebrova—ZEH-broh-vah

PHRASES

Pasy, prosim—PAH-see PROH-seem
Dve piva—DVYEH PEE-vah
Dobrou notz—DOH-broh NOHTS
Ano—AH-noh
R-U-S-T-Y—AIR OO EHSS TEH EEP-see-lohn
PREE-vehz-lee ZHVEE-kahen-kee ah TSEE-gah-reh-tee
PREE-vehz-lee YEH-nohm POOL KOO-froo ZHVEE-gah-
    chehk ah TSEE-gah-reht
NEH, toh bee-lah VEE-stah-vah z BRAH-tee-slah-vee
HOO-dehb-nyee NAH-stroh-yeh MAH-meh veh SKLAH-
    doo
DAH-leh
STOH-ee! STOH-ee, VOHR
BEE-struh! sahm-NOH-ee!
PREE-shehl sehs POH-dyee-vaht, KOH-cheech-koh?
SLEE-sheesh M'NYEH?
YEH too NYEGH-doh?
yah-see sehm POHSS-lyehd-nyee.
yah-ee sehm POHSS-lyehd-nyee ohd HEET-leh-rohf
    skeex. TSOO-pehr-mah-noo nah ROO-skee ZEH-mee
PROH-meeny (uh) (The "uh" is miuiscule.)
TO yeh yeh-ho OHB-lee-beh-neh SLOH-voh
VOHD-koo, PROH-seem.

TSEH-loh FLAHSH-koo
DYEH-koo-yoo
ROOM proh LAHNG-groh-vee KAH-mah-rah-dee!
YAH neh sehm KOH-moh-nee-stah yah-ee sehm yehn
  DYEHL-neek
AH-leh veem veets NEHSH MOO-ee-SHEFF

PRONUNCIATIONS

r	a tip of the tongue trill
x	as in German "a*ch*"
zh	as in G*i*g*i* *g*enre bei*g*e
sh	wi*sh*
ch	wi*tch*
ng	si*ng* si*n*k
g	*g*o
ee	not so tight as American
eh	not so lazy as American
oh	between our "oh" and "aw"
rzh	as in "J*iri*"-GOOD LUCK!
s	*s*o
z	*z*oo